# *The Poison of Jealousy*

Zafarullah

**The Poison of Jealousy**

Author: Zafarullah

**A Tribute to My Teacher and Mentor:**

**Sir Abdul Nafi:** Former Teacher, Currently Serving as Education Officer in Qail Abdullah Pakistan.

**Sir Syed Kaleem Shah:** Former District Education Officer, Currently Divisional Director Loralai Division Pakistan

## Preface

In every corner of the world, from bustling cities to remote villages, jealousy is a constant pressure, silently damaging the well-being of individuals, families and societies. It is an emotion that is regularly dismissed as part of human nature, yet its negative electricity is clear. Jealousy, in its midst, is a poison that silently enters our hearts, distorts our thoughts, creates cracks in our relationships, and social destruction.

This e-book, "The Poison of Envy," seeks to delve deeper into the nature of this powerful emotion, exploring its origins, manifestations, and far-reaching consequences on every individual and collective. Through research, scholarly insights, and spiritual teachings, we aim to understand envy in all its forms—whether it stems from a lack of trust, comparison, or fear—and examine how it causes harm to ourselves and society at large. By identifying the signs of envy, understanding the roots of this toxic emotion, and learning how to break free from its grip, we can empower ourselves to create healthier, more fulfilling lives.

I hope that through this e-book, readers will be able to capture the envy within them, take important steps to rid themselves of its influence, and ultimately build more harmony and groups. As we journey through the chapters, we can discover different perspectives, from mental theories and academic debates to religious and theological teachings, to shed light on this harmful pressure.

The goal is not always to capture envy, but to provide sensible tools and strategies to combat it and guide those who are prone to it in the direction of peace and emotional freedom. Envy, when left unchecked, can ruin homes, break friendships, and prevent non-public fulfillment. However, with self-awareness, compassion, and the courage to confront this emotion, we will break free from its grip and live lives full of joy, gratitude, and true fulfillment.

**About the Author**

Zafarullah is a writer, student, and passionate advocate for emotional well-being. With a deep interest in human psychology and secular development, Zafarullah has dedicated a significant portion of his existence to studying the complex emotions that govern human behavior. His paintings aim to bridge the gap between psychological research and religious knowledge, providing readers with insight into the path to living a healthier, more balanced life. After witnessing firsthand the devastating consequences of envy on individuals and groups, Zafarullah embarked on a journey to understand this emotion in more depth. Through years of study, self-reflection, and conversations with professionals in a variety of fields, he has come to recognize the fact that overcoming envy begins with self-awareness and the development of emotional intelligence. Zafarullah's writings touch on topics including personal improvement, emotional health, and spiritual growth. Through this e-book, he hopes to offer readers the tools they need to grasp, confront, and heal from envy, ultimately developing a more peaceful and harmonious world.

**Table of Contents**

**1. Introduction: The Silent Destroyer** — Understanding Jealousy the Nature of Jealousy Why Jealousy is More Than Just a Passing Emotion.

**2. The Psychology of Jealousy:** What Makes Us Feel Jealous? Evolutionary and Psychological Causes Jealousy as a Response to Insecurity and Fear

**3. The Roots of Jealousy:** Early Experiences and Personal History Study of Adolescence How Jealousy Tendencies Shape the Impact of Past Trauma on Jealousy

**4. Jealousy and Self-Esteem:** The Link Between Insecurity and Jealousy Creating a Healthy Experience of Low Self-Esteem as a Breeding Destination for Jealousy

**5. Religious Teachings on Jealousy:** Insights from Beliefs and Scriptures Islam, Christianity, Judaism, and Buddhism on Jealousy the Moral and Religious Consequences of Jealousy

**6. Jealousy and Society:** How This Emotion Destroys Communities Social Impacts of Jealousy on Families, Families, and Offices Cultural Influences on the Normalization of Jealousy

**7. The Jealous Mindset:** How to Recognize the Signs of Jealousy Identifying Jealousy in Yourself and Others Common Behavioral and Thought Patterns of Jealousy People

**8. Jealousy and Relationships:** How It Destroys Love and Trust the Corrosive Consequences of Jealousy on Romantic Relationships Navigating Jealousy in the Sphere of Friendship and Kinship Dynamics

**9. The Impact of Jealousy on Health:** The Mind-Body Connection How Jealousy Shows Up Physically Stress, Tension, and Frustration Are Linked to Jealousy

**10. Is Jealousy a Habit of Unsuccessful People?** The Link Between Jealousy and Personal Stagnation - How Jealousy Undermines Progress and Success.

**11. The role of comparison in jealousy:** Why we can't stop the perception of social evaluation and competition in the trap of jealousy Breaking unfastened from wanting to compete with others

**12. The danger of jealousy in professional life:** How jealousy kills careers Jealousy within the business space and its impact on professional success Overcoming jealousy among colleagues and superiors

**13. Spiritual treatment of jealousy:** Searching for inner peace and contentment Spiritual exercises to deal with jealousy Meditation, gratitude and self-reflection

**14. Healing from jealousy**: Steps towards emotional freedom Practical strategies to overcome jealousy the importance of forgiveness and self-compassion

**15. Raising awareness:** Teaching children how to deal with jealousy. Parenting strategies for dealing with jealousy in children - Creating a healthy emotional environment at the home level

**16. The Role of Empathy in Overcoming Jealousy** How Empathy and Knowledge Reduce Jealousy Developing Emotional Intelligence

**17. Jealousy in the Digital Age**: The Rise of Social Media and Jealousy How Social Media Fuels Jealousy Navigating the Virtual World without Being Jealous

**18. The Power of Gratitude:** Turning Jealousy into Appreciation How Practicing Gratitude Can Neutralize Jealousy Shifting Identity from Lack to Abundance

**19. Jealousy in Marriage:** Keeping Bonds Strong The Negative Role of Jealousy in Marriages Maintaining Trust, Transparency, and Verbal Exchange

**20. Overcoming Jealousy:** A Path to Personal Growth Turning Jealousy into a Catalyst for Self-Improvement - Building Resilience and Emotional Energy

**21. Collective Healing:** How to Create Jealousy-Free Communities the Importance of Collective Emotional Health - Building Supportive and Non-Aggressive Social Structures

**22. Conclusion: Letting Go of the Poison**—Living a Life Free of Jealousy Summary of Key Takeaways A Lifelong Adventure of Recovering from Jealousy

## Chapter 1: Introduction: Silent Destruction —
**Understanding Jealousy.** The Nature of Jealousy .Why Jealousy is more Than Just a Passing Emotion. Jealousy is one of the most insidious and damaging emotions a person can experience. It creeps into our lives uninvited, often taking root within the most intimate elements of our psyche, and without careful attention, it manages to slowly erode our relationships, mental health, and shared happiness. Unlike anger or unhappiness, jealousy has a way of sneaking up on us—often left unaddressed until it has already caused greater damage. It can be difficult to catch in its early stages because it often disguises itself as a simple feeling of dissatisfaction, envy, or

disappointment. However, left unchecked, jealousy can become a powerful force to destroy everything in its path. In this chapter, we will examine the nature of jealousy, how it manifests, why it is more than just a passing emotion, and the way it affects not only the person reporting it but also the people around them.

We will learn about its mental, emotional, and social dimensions, its origins, root causes, and its impact on the lives and relationships of men and women.

By the end of this chapter, readers will benefit from a clearer understanding of jealousy and why it is important to deal with it before it gets out of hand.

1. **The Nature of Jealousy**: Jealousy is an intense emotion that arises when we see the value of something threatened—whether it is a dating relationship, our social reputation, or a material possession. It is often described as a complex combination of anxiety, insecurity, and resentment. At its core, jealousy arises when we feel that something or a person we care about is responsible for being taken or passed on by someone else.
This sense of loss, or the potential for loss, triggers an emotional response that can range from mild discomfort to intense anger.

**Key characteristics of jealousy:**

**Emotional complexity:**

Jealousy is not a simple feeling. It includes a wide variety of emotions, including worry, envy, anger, and sadness. It can be as simple as a lack of love for a partner, resentment toward a partner's success, or frustration about the perceived unfairness of another person's life.

**Perceived threat:** The emotion is often motivated by a valuable opportunity that we value. This could be a relationship, fame, success, or reputation. The key is that the threat feels real, despite the fact that it is only imagined or exaggerated.

**Comparative nature:**

Jealousy is often born of comparison. It thrives in an environment where individuals measure their worth against others, whether consciously or unconsciously. This comparative mindset can magnify even the minor differences, and jealousy thrives on these perceived imbalances

2. **Why Jealousy Is More Than Just a Passing Emotion.** At first glance, jealousy may seem like a temporary emotional reaction—a fleeting feeling of discomfort that will pass over time. However, when examined more deeply, jealousy is much more than a passing emotion.

It is a persistent, often corrosive force that can have a profound impact on one's behavior and conduct, with lasting consequences. The Longevity of Jealousy:

**Chronic Nature:** While many emotions—like happiness or disappointment—fade away over time, jealousy can linger long after its initial cause. It can become a lasting legacy emotion, influencing thoughts and actions long after the event or situation that triggered it. Over time, this lingering feeling of jealousy can cause changes in how one perceives one's relationships, achievements, or even self-worth.

**Impact on Identity:** When jealousy is left unchecked, it begins to shape one's identity. A person who feels resentful on a regular basis may begin to see him or herself as less capable, less attractive, or less valuable than others do. These feelings can erode self-esteem, leading to a diminished sense of well-being and a persistent sense of inadequacy.

**Behavioral consequences:**

The longer jealousy is allowed to persist, the more it can affect behavior.

A jealous character can become controlling, manipulative, or passive-aggressive, which alienates others and damages relationships. Jealousy has the potential to change how we interact with those we care about most, whether through dispassionate actions or outright hostility. Cognitive distortions caused by jealousy:

**Overestimation of risks:** Jealousy regularly results in cognitive distortions—irrational thinking patterns that inflate perceived risks. For example, someone may interpret a partner's harmless verbal exchange with another person as a sign of romantic infatuation, even when there is no evidence to support the assumption.

This type of thinking fuels anxiety and leads to unnecessary fighting.

**Blame and Projection:**

Jealous individuals regularly project their insecurities onto others.

For example, a person who feels inferior to their partner may accuse them of being dishonest or manipulative, even when no such behavior is occurring. The tendency to blame others for one's own emotional struggles can make it difficult to resolve jealousy in a positive way.

3. **Roots of Jealousy:** Why Do We Feel It? Jealousy does not just come out of nowhere. It is often rooted deep in our private history, psychology, and social context. To fully recognize jealousy, we need to explore its origins and the underlying elements that ensure that individuals are more susceptible to experiencing it.
4. **Psychological factors**:

**Insecurity and low self-esteem:**

One of the primary drivers of jealousy is deep-seated insecurity or a lack of self-confidence. People who are unsure of themselves or their abilities tend to compare themselves to others and feel threatened when others dominate or get the attention. Jealousy, on this feeling, acts as a defense mechanism — an emotional response to protect one's fragile sense of self.

**Fear of abandonment:** For those who have mastered abandonment or further betrayal — whether through early life neglect, failed relationships, or mistrust — the system of jealousy fears that the story will repeat itself.

This anxiety results in hyper vigilance and multiple possibilities for sensing threats where none may exist.

**Attachment styles:**

Our attachment patterns — the behavioral styles we develop in our early relationships with caregivers — can greatly influence our ability to deal with jealousy. People with insecure attachment styles (such as neurotic or avoidant attachment) may be at increased risk for jealousy because they have mixed feelings and lack emotional security.

**Cultural and Sociocultural Influences:** Social Comparison: We live in a world that constantly encourages comparison.

From social media to aggressive work environments, we are surrounded by opportunities to measure ourselves against others. This constant contrast can fuel jealousy, as can our ability to determine what we do not do.

**Cultural Expectations:** In many cultures, there are specific social norms and expectations regarding success, beauty, and wealth. These external pressures can fuel feelings of inadequacy, leading people to envy individuals who meet cultural ideals. The more someone feels they fall short of these social standards, the more likely they are to indulge in jealousy.

**4. Jealousy in Relationships**:

Jealousy often arises in close relationships—whether romantic, familial, or platonic. In these relationships, jealousy can escalate quickly and cause great harm if left unchecked.

**Romantic Jealousy Possessiveness and Control:**

In romantic relationships, jealousy can manifest as possessiveness.

A person may try to regulate their partner's actions, limit their interactions with others, or monitor their behavior to reduce feelings of jealousy. This behavior stems from a fear of losing their partner's love to people. However, it can quickly escalate into controlling tendencies that undermine the relationship.

**Trust Issues:**

Jealousy often stems from a lack of consideration. If there is no aphanasceticism within the relationship, they will constantly question the other person's loyalty for no solid reason.

This can create a toxic cycle of suspicion and defensiveness that damages the connection in the end.

**Family Jealousy:**

**Sibling Rivalry:** Jealousy can also manifest itself in your own family dynamics, especially among siblings. Competition for interests and assets can lead to jealousy, especially if one sibling feels that the other is favored or has extra popularity.
**Parental Jealousy:** In some cases, parents may feel jealous of their child's success, especially if they experience that the child is surpassing them in career, achievements, or recognition, as well as in areas.

This can create resentment and hinder the development of a healthy, mature child's marriage.

## 5. Social and societal effects of jealousy.

Jealousy does not only affect individuals but also has an impact on communities and societies. When left unchecked, jealousy can contribute to discord, deep divisions, and a culture of opposition and resentment.

**In the workplace:**

Undermining success: Jealousy is a major problem in professional settings.

Employees who are jealous of a colleague's success may also try to sabotage their efforts, spread gossip, or undermine their achievements. Strained relationships in friendships and social circles: Jealousy can create tension in friendships, especially when one friend considers another more successful, attractive, or popular. It can lead to passive competitive behavior, secret resentment, and ultimately the breakdown of friendships. Jealousy is not just an emotion—it is a silent destroyer that can undermine our health, break up relationships, and disrupt entire communities. Understanding the nature of jealousy, recognizing its root causes, and acknowledging its potential to cause harm is the first step toward recovery. The chapters that follow will explore how to manage, conquer, and ultimately heal from jealousy, providing realistic techniques and insights for breaking free from its negative grip.

By confronting jealousy, we can, on the contrary, create a being free from resentment, resentment, and lack of trust.

## Chapter 2: The Psychology of Jealousy—What Makes Us Feel Jealous.

Jealousy is a complex emotional experience, deeply rooted in our mental makeup. While it is regularly observed without any negative force, information about its origins and the mechanisms that underlie why we enjoy it in the first place is scant.

Feelings of envy and jealousy are not simply random or temporary reactions to external opportunities. Alternatively, however, they are rooted in fundamental components of human nature.

To understand the cause of envy, we must uncover the underlying reactions and explore the evolutionary and psychological explanations for this powerful emotion.

In this chapter, we explore why envy exists from both an evolutionary and a psychological perspective. We will discuss how feelings of insecurity and anxiety lead to envy and the ways in which these emotions become entrenched in our minds. By examining the roots of envy, we can begin to understand how it affects human behavior, relationships, and social dynamics.

**Evolutionary Explanations of Envy**

From an evolutionary perspective, envy can be viewed as a survival mechanism. In early human records, envy evolved as a response to perceived threats, mating opportunities, and social bonds—all-important factors for survival and reproduction. While the context of modern life has changed, those basic instincts are deeply embedded in human nature. Thus, jealousy is rooted in the desire to preserve and protect relationships, which can be important for survival and reproduction. Even in the absence of direct threats, feelings of jealousy serve as a precautionary device, signaling at least a potential threat to one's relationship with a partner or access to resources.

**2. Resource Conservation:**

Competition and Status Jealousy is also a form of opposition to withheld assets, whether they are friends, fame, wealth, or social influence.

Humans are deeply social creatures, and much of our psychological wiring is designed to navigate complex social hierarchies.

In tribal or social organization settings, individuals compete for interest, energy, and status. Jealousy arises when someone perceives that another character has a bonus, especially in the context of relationships or popularity within a group.

**Social comparison:** According to evolutionary psychologists, social evaluation is a key factor in jealousy.

Early humans lived in corporations and their survival depended not only on fairness but also on social status within the organization.

The choice of Cresson's work in reserve within the organization would have generated envy when others surpassed or influenced them. However, it can be determined in modern social environments where humans feel envy of the success, prestige, or wealth of others.

**Status Envy:**

**Research** suggests that envy also arises when people feel threatened by someone who appears to have more resources, better opportunities, or a higher social status. In early human tribes, access to resources, including food, shelter, and friends, was often dependent on one's social status.

A jealous response became a motivation when one individual's advancement was seen as detrimental to another's chances of survival or fulfillment. This evolutionary response is seen today in specialized environments or exceptionally competitive social environments.

These evolutionary elements of envy, rooted in competition and the protection of important assets, help explain why people are predisposed to feel envy when faced with perceived threats to their social or intimate relationships.

**Psychological explanations of envy**

While evolutionary psychology provides us with insight into the origins of envy, modern psychology offers a more specific view of the ways in which it operates in the human mind. Jealousy is not always just an automatic, instinctive reaction - it's also shaped by private experiences, psychological states and social dynamics.

1. **Jealousy as a Response to Insecurity**
   According to Autoscore, jealousy regularly arises from feelings of lack of confidence. When we feel uncertain about our worth or worry that we are not measuring up in some area of life, jealousy can arise as a response to our fear of those around us.
   **Low self-esteem:** People who struggle with low self-esteem are more prone to jealousy. If someone does not experience more stability in their area, they will perceive others as a threat to their identity, success or relationships. For example, if a person feels that they are "not good enough anymore", they may become jealous of someone they perceive as more attractive, more successful or more accomplished.
   This fear of inadequacy gives rise to feelings of jealousy.
   **Fear of abandonment:** People with attachment insecurity, along with those with a disruptive attachment style, may be associated with a deep fear of abandonment. People who are skilled at initial emotional neglect or infrequent care giving are more likely to feel threatened by the looks or affection that they receive from others, especially from a romantic partner.

This worry about being left behind or replaced whenever someone else enters the picture leads to a strong emotional response of jealousy.

Personal insecurity in social or professional contexts in professional settings, jealousy often stems from insecurity about one's abilities or achievements.

A man or woman may become jealous of a partner's success, not necessarily because of what the partner has done, but because it highlights the loss of their own lifestyle success.

This form of jealousy may be rooted in feelings of inadequacy or a concern about being left behind in one's career.

2. **Jealousy and Fear:**

The Role of Anxiety Jealousy is mostly a response to underlying anxiety.

Fear—whether it's the fear of failure, the fear of being left out, or the fear of being left behind—plays a major role in giving rise to jealousy.

Intrusive thoughts are constantly scanning for threats to one's ability, and jealousy is one of the ways the mind reacts when it feels a commitment to something valuable.

**Fear of losing what we have:** A basic fear that drives jealousy upward is the fear of loss.

It might be the worry of losing a romantic partner to someone else, losing credibility in a social institution, or losing one's job to a more capable competitor.

This anxiety leads to feelings of jealousy because thoughts will become fixed on the perceived threat to one's experience of security.

**Fear of not measuring up:** Another anxiety that often gives rise to jealousy is the fear of inadequacy. When another person seems more attractive, attractive, or capable, this can lead to feelings of jealousy due to a deep-seated fear of being "less" than others are. This is especially true in clearly competitive environments where people are constantly measuring themselves against their friends.

**Fear of exclusion:**
Jealousy can also arise from concerns about social exclusion.
People have a natural need to belong, and when they perceive that another person is taking notice or affection in their social circle or romantic partner, feelings of jealousy and a fear of being fake can emerge.

3. **Cognitive distortions**:
   How we fuel jealousy. Cognitive distortions — irrational ways of thinking that exaggerate or distort reality — are key mental elements in jealousy. These mental filters can lead someone to interpret neutral or ambiguous situations in a very frighteningly mildly plausible way, thus fueling feelings of jealousy.

   **Catastrophizing:**
   This is the tendency to expect the worst-case scenario. For example, a jealous person may also mechanically expect that their partner's friendship with sexual partners will inevitably lead to infidelity, even though there is no evidence to support this concern.
   Destructive jealousy heightens the emotional intensity of jealousy, making the person overreact and unable to really think.

   **Mind Reading:**
   Another common cognitive distortion in jealousy is "thought analysis," in which someone assumes they know what others are thinking.
   For example, a person may assume that their partner is no longer interested in them because they are spending time with someone else, despite the fact that there is no indication that this is true.
   These irrational assumptions provide additional justification for jealousy, even when there is little evidence to support them.

**All-or-nothing thinking:**
Jealous people often see situations in black and white terms in which the success or attention of one man or woman automatically comes at the expense of another.
This kind of wonder fails to account for the complexities of relationships and social dynamics, and it can lead to useless jealousy in situations that are not inherently threatening.
Overall, jealousy is an emotion with deep evolutionary and psychological roots. From an evolutionary perspective, jealousy evolved as a survival mechanism to defend resources, relationships, and reproductive possibilities. Psychologically, it is often brought on by feelings of insecurity and fear.
Specifically, the fear of loss, failure, and exclusion. Understanding these underlying factors can help us understand when jealousy arises and why it can be so difficult to control.

# Chapter 3: The Roots of Jealousy –

Early Experiences and Personal History Jealousy is not an emotion that fully emerges in adulthood. Rather, it is often rooted in early adolescent assessments and the way in which our primary caregivers, siblings, and the broader social environment shape our state.

Our past, especially our childhood, plays a significant role in shaping the system of feelings like jealousy and the way we react to perceived threats in relationships and social situations. Unresolved childhood stories, attachment patterns, and early traumas can leave lasting impressions on the way we cope with jealousy in adulthood. We will explore how early adolescent experiences influence jealous behaviors, focusing on the role of parental relationships, sibling dynamics, and attachment styles.

We may even look at how past traumas—whether emotional, physical, or relational—can profoundly influence our ability to accept our own truths, form healthy relationships, and manipulate feelings of jealousy. Non-public history, we are able to begin the process of healing and changing these deep emotional patterns.

1. How childhood experiences shape jealousy tendencies. Childhood is the art of our emotional lives. The experiences we have during our childhood—especially in our relationships with caregivers, siblings, and peers—can have a profound impact on our emotional responses as adults. Jealousy is one of the emotions that can be found in our earliest interactions with others.

   **The Parental Influence:** Attachment and Emotional Security The attachment theory, advanced by John Bowlby and Mary Erworth, suggests that emotional bonds formed between infants and their caregivers shape how people relate to others throughout their lives. In addition, this plays a key role in how we experience feelings like jealousy.

**Secure Attachment:**

Children who enjoy consistent, loving care from their caregivers typically develop a "stable attachment" style. These children learn that their wishes will be met and they grow up with a sense of agreement and emotional security. Securely attached individuals are much less likely to experience excessive jealousy because their relationships have a strong foundation of self-esteem and trust. They are generally more trusting and happy with emotional closeness, because they have discovered that others can be reliable and supportive.

**Insecure attachment:**

On the other hand, adolescents who are overcome by conflict, neglect, or excessive care may also develop "insecure attachment styles." There are several types of insecure attachment, each of which is associated with a specific expression of jealousy:

**Distracted attachment:** Children who experience a disruptive attachment may feel uncertain about their relationships.

They may be conflicted by the fear of abandonment and develop a fear of being changed. As a result, they may experience jealousy in adulthood in response to perceived threats to their relationships. They may also be excessively jealous when their partner turns their attention to someone else or when they feel left out or ignored.

**Avoidant Attachment:**

Children with avoidant attachment tend to suppress their emotions and have a strong need for independence.

As adults, they will suppress feelings of jealousy, but that does not mean they are immune to it. They may become jealous in a more passive-competitive way, withdraw emotionally, or distance themselves from those who threaten them.

**Disorganized Attachment:**

Those with disorganized attachments tend to have chaotic, unpredictable relationships with caregivers. They often have mixed feelings about closeness and take it for granted, and their emotional responses can be erratic. In adolescence, this can manifest as unpredictable jealousy, swinging between excessive emotional response and emotional detachment. When a child experiences emotional neglect, rejection, or abandonment in childhood, this can sow the seeds of jealousy.

Lack of emotional security and protection in the early years can lead to intense feelings of vulnerability and a terrible anxiety about being left behind or replaced. Sibling rivalry and jealousy Sibling relationships are often the first place we study competition, evaluation, and jealousy.

Sibling competition—while a natural part of growing up—can become a major factor in the development of jealous tendencies if not handled in a healthy way.

**Liking and comparing:**

Feelings of jealousy can arise when one sibling consistently desires another.

Children may also compare themselves to their siblings and experience that they may no longer be as loved or liked.

For example, if an infant receives more attention, praise, or material rewards, the alternative sibling may develop feelings of resentment, inadequacy, and jealousy. These feelings can increase in adulthood, especially in relationships where a man or woman feels they are "competing" for attention, love, or success.

**Achievement or attention envy:**
Sibling jealousy can also arise when a sibling excels in a particular area, whether academically, socially, or in physical skills.

A young child who feels overshadowed by a more accomplished sibling may develop a lifelong sense of inadequacy, leading to feelings of envy later in life when faced with peer comparisons in paintings or social settings.

Trained young people study the importance of competition, fairness, and validation in their early relationships with siblings who regularly accompany them at some stage of maturity, influencing their feelings of envy in relationships and social contexts.

2. The impact of past trauma on envy trauma, especially early relational trauma, has a powerful impact on the way we enjoy and express envy in adulthood. Whether it is the ultimate result of physical abuse, emotional neglect, or the loss of a loved one, trauma can distort our perception of others, increasing deep fears of betrayal, abandonment, and loss and ourselves.

**Emotional Trauma:**
Fear of Insecurity and Rejection Emotional trauma, including being bullied, experiencing parental separation, or having a personality that is emotionally unavailable or abusive, can create lasting scars. These stories can result in deep-seated insecurities that fuel feelings of jealousy later in life. Individuals who have been emotionally traumatized may also develop a fear of abandonment and feel hypersensitive to perceived threats in their relationships.

**Fear of Abandonment:**
If a young child has a knack for being abandoned or loved by a caregiver (whether physically or

emotionally), they may develop abandonment anxiety that carries over into adulthood. As a result, they may interpret minor actions or behaviors of a partner, friend, or colleague as signs that they are deserted or about to change. This increased sensitivity to rejection of competence makes them more vulnerable to feelings of jealousy.

**Low self-esteem:**
Trauma can also leave individuals with a low sense of self-worth. When a young child experiences neglect or emotional abuse, they internalize the idea that they are unworthy of love. As they grow older, this internalized sense of inadequacy can make them more susceptible to jealousy. They may also feel threatened by others who they find more successful, attractive, or affectionate, believing that they themselves are not worthy of such lavish attention.

**Physical Abuse**:
Hyperactive vigilance and Mistrust Trauma, along with physical abuse, can have a profound impact on the ability to empathize with others. Victims of abuse may also develop a regular state of hyper vigilance, in which they are constantly on the lookout for potential threats. This hyper vigilance often manifests as jealousy in intimate relationships, as the individual will become overly suspicious of their partner's actions and intentions.

**Mistrust in Relationships**:
People who are abused struggle to empathize. They may also assume that everyone they are close to will eventually hurt or betray them, and that they will be hyper vigilant for any signs of betrayal. This heightened experience of distrust leads to jealousy, as the individual interprets innocent interactions or behaviors as signs and symptoms of potential infidelity or abandonment.

**Attachment issues:**
For those who have experienced physical or sexual trauma, attachment to others can be fraught with distress. These people may also have difficulty forming healthy, trusting relationships and may react to perceived emotional or physical closeness from others with jealousy or possessiveness. A deep-seated fear of being hurt again fuels some jealous feelings.

**Loss of a parent or significant relationship:**
Fear of change Loss, whether through death or abandonment, can be another form of early trauma that shapes jealousy. Children who rejoice when a parent or major caregiver dies may develop a heightened fear of being replaced, which can carry over into adult relationships.

**Grief and Emotional Loss:**
The loss of a committed or major caregiver can lead to feelings of deep sadness and lack of trust. As a result, people who have lost commitment early in life may also experience intense feelings of fear after forming new relationships, believing that they will eventually be replaced or abandoned by their partner, friends, or perhaps even by themselves. This fear of family replacement can manifest as jealousy without any problems, especially when their partner spends time with others or makes new connections.

3. **Treating Jealousy Tendencies Rooted in Childhood** and Trauma the good news is that jealousy, even if rooted in early year's experiences or trauma, can be cured with self-care and therapeutic intervention. Healing the wounds that contribute to jealousy requires recognizing the emotional triggers and working to address underlying insecurities and fears.

   **Treatment Methods:**
4. Cognitive Behavioral Therapy (CBT):CBT is an effective way to identify and address the cognitive

distortions that fuel jealousy. By changing irrational beliefs (such as "I'm not good enough anymore" or "I might be left out"), individualized scans reduce the intensity of feelings of jealousy.

**Attachment-based therapy:**
For people with attachment-related jealousy issues, attachment-based therapy can be beneficial. This form of therapy focuses on removing emotional scars caused by unhealthy, trusting relationships and insecurities.

**Childhood attachment Trauma-focused therapy:**
For those who have experienced traumatic experiences, trauma-targeted therapy with EMDR (eye movement desensitization and reprocessing) or somatic experiential learning can help to map and initiate emotional pain related to past trauma, reducing the fear and lack of trust that fuel jealousy. Jealousy, like many other emotional responses, is deeply rooted in our early reports.

Childhood emotional dynamics—whether through attachment style, sibling rivalry, or trauma—have a lasting impact on how we experience and manage jealousy as adults. Understanding these sources allows us to recognize the deeper emotional triggers that fuel jealousy and to bear the idea of addressing and treating these tendencies.

In the following chapters, we will explore how jealousy manifests in relationships and societies and provide sensible steps to overcome these unhelpful patterns in order to cultivate healthier, more trusting emotional lives.

By rehabilitating the roots of jealousy, we are able to loosen its grip and embody more stable, loving relationships with others and ourselves.

# Chapter 4: Jealousy and Self-Worth - The Connection between Insecurity and Jealousy

Jealousy is often deeply tied to one's sense of self-worth, at least in part. While the emotion can be triggered by outside circumstances—including perceived threats in relationships, or social situations—its depth and frequency are closely indicated by the way we feel about ourselves. When individuals struggle with a fragile sense of worthlessness or low self-esteem, jealousy becomes an almost automatic response to situations in which they perceive themselves as inadequate or inferior to others. Conversely, when we develop a strong, healthy sense of self-esteem, jealousy is significantly reduced. It explores the relationship between a lacks of confidence. In addition, jealousy, highlighting how low self-esteem can be a breeding ground for jealousy. We will even explore strategies for developing a more fit sense of self-esteem that can serve as a powerful antidote to jealousy.

1. **Low self-esteem as a breeding ground for envy.**
   Self-esteem refers to the way we perceive and value ourselves. It includes our beliefs, our abilities, our well-being, and our place in the world. When low self-esteem is low, individuals often feel inadequate, incompetent, or unable to achieve their goals or maintain healthy relationships.
   
   This internalized experience of inferiority complex can lead to jealousy. Typically, they encounter situations where they feel "less than" others.

The Role of Insecurity in Jealousy Insecurity stems from a loss of self-esteem or belief in one's abilities, appearance or worth. It often arises when we experience that we are not good enough or when we compare ourselves to others who have qualities, achievements, or relationships that we lack. This insecurity can create an emotional void, which jealousy seeks to fill.

**Comparing you to others:**
People with low self-esteem often evaluate themselves negatively in relation to others. When they perceive that someone else has something that they lack — whether it is a physical trait, an achievement, or an intimate history — they may feel jealous.
This inconsistency fuels their insecurity, leading them to agree that they are inadequate, unworthy, or incapable of meeting comparative fulfillment. In essence, jealousy becomes a mirror that reflects their personal feelings of self-doubt. Jealousy as the fear of losing something we do not feel we deserve:
Low self-esteem can also cause people to feel like they no longer deserve the good things in their lives.
As a result, when they see others achieving success, gaining love, or receiving attention, it triggers jealousy. In this case, jealousy stems from the worry about giving up something they do not feel they have the right to keep. They may worry that someone "better" will come along or will come along to take their partner's affections, their job, or their social status.

**Jealousy and validation:**
For many people, self-esteem depends on external validation—whether it's from a partner, friends, or colleagues. This can lead to jealousy, as they experience that their own worth is not being acknowledged or supported. In most of these instances, jealousy will become an emotional response that reflects deep insecurity about one's place in the international community.

Now it is no longer without a doubt what others have—it is usually what the person believes they themselves lack.

**The cycle of envy:** How low self-esteem fuels envy. Low self-esteem creates a vicious cycle where envy perpetuates feelings of worthlessness, which in turn creates additional envy. Here is how the cycle works:

**1. Feelings of inadequacy:**
The individual feels insecure about themselves, whether because of their appearance, abilities, social reputation, or relationships.

**2. Comparisons with others:**
They compare themselves to another person who has qualities or achievements they like, including the affection of a partner, the success of a colleague, or the recognition of a friend.

**3. Jealousy Reaction:**

This evaluation triggers feelings of envy — envy over what the alternative role lacks.

**4. Negative Self-Talk:**

Jealousy leads to a negative self-image, which increases feelings of inadequacy. For example, they will assume, "I will never be as attractive as they are," or "I am not good enough to achieve that."

**5. Increased Insecurity:**
Negative self-talk reinforces their insecurities and inferiority complex, which in turn increases their chances of feeling jealous of their destiny.

As the cycle continues, envy can become a persistent emotional state, and people may even struggle to break free from it until they address the underlying cause—the inferiority complex.

**2. Building a Healthy Sense of Self-Worth**
Fortunately, vanity is not fixed. It can be improved

through self-awareness, self-compassion, and planned effort. Building a healthy sense of self-worth can significantly reduce jealousy and allow people to navigate life with greater emotional resilience, confidence, and satisfaction.

Cultivating self-awareness the first step in building a healthy self-worth is to pay attention to oneself. This means taking the time to explore one's thoughts, feelings, and behaviors in a nonjudgmental way. Self-awareness enables people to understand when jealousy is rising and what the underlying causes are—whether they are rooted in a lack of confidence, worry, or self-worth.

**Mindfulness techniques**: Mindfulness is a technique that encourages people to observe their own thoughts and feelings without judgment.

By practicing mindfulness, people can become more aware of when jealousy arises and how they respond to it. This awareness allows them to choose a more constructive response instead of being swept away by negative feelings.

**Journaling:**
Writing down thoughts and feelings can help individuals gain beneficial insight into their insecurities and self-doubt. Through journaling, they can uncover their emotional reaction patterns, catch the triggers of jealousy, and begin to reframe the negative mindset.

Adopting self-compassion: Self-compassion means presenting themselves with the same kindness and skill that a close friend would present. –

**Recognition. Self-compassionate self-talk**:
Instead of criticizing themselves for feeling jealous or inadequate, people can practice self-compassionate self-talk.

For example, if jealousy arises, they can tell themselves, "its okay to feel this way. These feelings do not define me. I am worthy and enough, just as I am." This helps break the cycle of negative self-talk that regularly accompanies jealousy.

**Forgiving you:**

People with low self-esteem often dwell on their mistakes and insecurities, believing that they are not worthy of success or happiness. Learning to forgive themselves for mistakes is an important part of building self-worth.

By moving beyond guilt or shame, people can free themselves from the emotional weight that fuels jealousy. Shifting the focus from comparing yourself to others to focusing on those who excel at non-public growth and self-improvement.

People with healthy self-esteem understand that they don't have to be "better" than everyone else to be valuable—they certainly want to be a satisfying example of themselves. Setting personal goals: Instead of mastering what others have or are doing, individuals can set their own personal goals. This could include improving a skill, pursuing a passion, or investing in personal development. By taking steps toward these desires, people feel empowered and are less likely to feel jealous of others' successes.

**Practicing gratitude:**

Focusing on what you lack can help reduce feelings of envy. Practicing gratitude helps individuals recognize their own blessings and strengths. By frequently reflecting on the positive elements in their personal lives, individuals can develop a sense of satisfaction and appreciation for who they can be. Rather than viewing the successes of others as a threat, people with a healthy sense of self are able to enjoy the successes of others without feeling deprived.

Developing an abundance mindset, in which there is enough fulfillment, love, and opportunity for all of us, can help people experience a sense of stability in their own self-worth.

**Celebrate the success of others:**

Building healthy relationships and boundaries Insecure people often struggle with jealousy in relationships because they worry about rejection, loss, or being replaced. Building healthy relationships requires setting clear boundaries and trusting others to recognize them. Healthy relationships, both romantic and platonic, are based entirely on mutual respect, open verbal exchange, and consideration rather than opposition or ownership. Being able to communicate needs and boundaries and setting boundaries is essential in relationships.

By actually saying what is acceptable and what is not always acceptable, individuals create an environment of agreement, in which jealousy is less likely to arise.

**Trust in Yourself and Others:**

One of the foundations of healthy self-esteem is trust in yourself and others. In your ability to handle challenges in relationships without resorting to jealousy or possessiveness.

**3.** The Role of Positive Affirmations in Reinforcing Self-Worth Positive affirmations are another effective tool for building self-esteem. They are quick, high-quality statements that individuals can repeat to themselves to challenge negative beliefs and reinforce positive self-concepts.

**Examples of positive affirmations:**

"I am worthy of love and appreciation."

"I believe in making the right choices for myself."

"I am enough, just as I am."

"I have unique traits that make me valuable."

By repeating these affirmations often, people can reprogram their brains to give themselves extra credit and reassurance, making them less vulnerable to jealousy. Jealousy is often rooted in deep insecurity and a lack of self-worth.

When we experience inadequacy or unworthiness, we are more likely to compare ourselves to others and feel threatened by their fulfillment, love, or attention.

However, by cultivating self-awareness, embracing self-compassion, and focusing on self-improvement, we can develop a healthy sense of self-worth that serves as a powerful defense against jealousy.

The process of improving the void is ongoing, but with continued effort, it is possible to transform the rightness of jealousy into personal growth, emotional resilience, and increased happiness.

# Chapter 5: Religious Teachings on Envy:

Insights from Beliefs and Scriptures, I comment on Christianity, Judaism, and Buddhism on envy. The Moral and Secular Consequences of Envy.

Envy is a deeply human emotion that transcends cultural and spiritual barriers. In certain conceptual systems, envy is considered a flawed and negative emotion, one that can lead individuals away from secular exaltation and moral virtue. Most major world religions understand the dangerous consequences of envy, provide teachings and guidance on how to overcome it, nurture higher levels of emotion, and agree with others.

Here, we explore views on envy from 4 of the most influential religions in the field: Islam, Christianity, Judaism, and Buddhism. Each of these traditions offers a unique perspective on the roots of envy, its consequences, and the religious practices that can help individuals overcome this unpleasant emotion.

1. **Islam and Envy:**
   Protection from Dangerous Emotions Envy (also known as "hasd") in Islam is considered one of the most dangerous emotions that can harm every man or woman and society. The Quran and the Hadith (sayings of the Prophet of Islam) offer clear guidance on the negative nature of envy and how Muslims can defend against it. The Quran and Envy the Quran mentions envy in several contexts, condemning it as a negative emotion that can result in jealousy, hatred, and dangerous actions.
   This highlights how envy led to the downfall of important figures in Islamic history, along with the envy of Iblis (Satan) close to Adam. Iblis's jealousy and arrogance led

to Adam's refusal to bow down to him, leading to his fall from grace.

One of the most excellent Quranic references to envy appears in Surah Al-Falaq (113:5), where it states "The envious seeks a safe haven from the evil of the envious while he is envious."

This verse acknowledges the harmful nature of envy and jealousy, encouraging Muslims to seek protection from its evil consequences through prayer and seeking refuge in Allah.

Another important reference is Surah Al-Qasas (28:76-82), in which envy is described as a wealthy man who is arrogant because of his wealth and standing. His envy and complacency led to his eventual downfall, which shows the destructive power of envy.

**Hadiths and Envy**

The Hadith emphasize that envy is now harmful not only to the person who possesses it but also to those around them. The Prophet (peace and blessings of Allah be upon him) has warned against envy in several sayings:

"Beware! There is a disease of the coronary heart called "envy" (hasd). It destroys your righteous deeds, just as a stove destroys wood." (Sunan Abu Dawood)

"Now do not be green with envy of one another, now do not hate one another, do not cut off one another, and do not turn away from one another." (Sahih Muslim)

In these sayings, the Prophet (peace and blessings of Allah be upon him) highlighted that envy can destroy one's spiritual and moral integrity, leading to bad behaviors such as hatred, division, and resentment.

Instead, Islam encourages individuals to be grateful, content, and to believe that Allah's will is always just.

**Moral and Spiritual Consequences of Envy in Islam**

In Islam, envy can lead to many moral and spiritual consequences:

1. **Spiritual impurity:** Envy can corrupt the heart, making it difficult to extend sincere love and compassion to others.
2. **Destruction of good deeds:** As mentioned in the hadiths, envy can damage one's noble deeds, just as a stove consumes wood. It can extinguish high-level acts of worship, kindness, and sincerity.
3. **Social discord:** Envy often ends in jealousy, competition, and struggle. In communities, it can cause division, distrust, and chaos.
4. **Distrust in Allah's plan:** Envy can reflect a lack of agreement in the awareness of Allah. This means that an individual is disappointed with the benefits or opportunities granted by Allah and resents the success or benefits of others.

To combat envy, Muslims are encouraged to be content (rida) with Allah's will. Instead of dwelling on bad feelings, pray for the fulfillment and blessing of others.

2. **Christianity and Envy:**

A Call to Love and Humility in Christianity, envy is also seen as a sin and an unpleasant emotion that can damage love, peace, and team spirit.

The teachings of Jesus Christ, in addition to the letters of the apostle Paul, provide guidance on how Christians can overcome envy and cultivate virtues including love, humility, and gratitude.

**The Bible and Envy**

In the New Testament, envy is always presented as an undesirable and sinful emotion. The apostle Paul wrote about envy in his letters, urging Christians to avoid it and live in harmony with others.

"Where envy and selfish ambition are, there you will find corruption and every evil practice." (James 3:16)

"Let us not become conceited, provoking and envying one another."

(Galatians 5:26) "Love is patient; love is kind; it does not envy; it does not boast; it is not puffed up."

(1 Corinthians 13:13)3) These passages emphasize that envy, which is rooted in selfishness and pleasure, leads to disease and strife, while love and humility lead to peace and harmony.

The Bible encourages Christians to be aware of cultivating love, forgiveness, and compassion rather than envy or jealousy.

## Moral and Spiritual Consequences of Jealousy in Christianity

In Christian teachings, jealousy can have both moral and secular consequences:

**1. Separation from God's Love: Jealousy** is seen as a form of sin that separates people from God's love and way.

**2. Disrupting Relationships:** It leads to jealousy. Bitterness and fighting destroy relationships. Jesus' teachings emphasize reconciliation and harmony, and jealousy is seen as an obstacle to both.

3. **Obstruction of Spiritual Growth:** Jealousy hinders religious growth. It takes one's identity away from gratitude and humility and places it on flawed emotions. This can prevent the believer from developing Christlike qualities. To overcome envy, Christians are exhorted to use virtues such as humility, love, perseverance, and contentment, trusting that God's plans for their lives are true.

**3. Judaism and Envy:**

A Warning against Envy and Greed Judaism also warns against envy, emphasizing the importance of gratitude and contentment with what God has provided. Jewish scriptures, especially the Torah, highlight the negative power of envy and the importance of cultivating a generous and compassionate spirit.

The Torah and Envy There are several passages in the Torah that address envy and jealousy:

"You shall not covet your neighbor's dwelling. You shall not covet your neighbor's wife, or his male servant, or his female servant, or his ox, or his donkey, or anything that is your neighbor's." (Exodus 20:17)

This commandment, part of the Ten Commandments, categorically forbids coveting or desiring things that belong to others, which is the core of envy. The act of coveting is considered a violation of faith in God's provision, encouraging people to be aware of their own benefits in preference to what others have.

**Wisdom Literature and Envy The book of Proverbs offers several insights into the dangers of envy:**

"A heart at peace gives life to the flesh, but envy rots the bones." (Proverbs 14:30)

"Do not let your heart envy sinners, but be zealous for the fear of the Lord in general." (Proverbs 23:17)

Envy and jealousy are seen as negative forces that erode one's spirit, leading to physical and emotional degradation. Proverbs teaches that a nonviolent heart, rooted in the concern for the Lord and contentment with one's circumstances, is beneficial at some distance.

**Moral and Spiritual Consequences of Envy in Judaism**

Envy in Judaism is seen as a destructive force that ends in.

**1. Spiritual Decay:** Envy fosters bitterness and resentment, which can weaken one's relationships with God and others. **2. Moral Corruption**: Coveting the property of others can lead to immoral behavior: dishonesty, theft, or deceit.

4. **Disrupting Community Harmony:**

Envy can create divisions within a network, leading to strife and fighting. Judaism encourages individuals to focus on gratitude for the blessings they have and to avoid coveting the things of others, to cultivate contentment, and to reflect on God's provision.

**4. Buddhism and Envy:**

A Poison of the Mind In Buddhism, envy is considered one of the three poisons—along with greed and lack of knowledge—that bind individuals to the struggle (samsara). Buddhism teaches that envy arises from attachment and the mistaken belief that there is never enough happiness or fulfillment to go around. A deeply rooted mental torment distorts one's belief in reality and contributes to suffering.

**Buddhist Teachings on Envy**

Buddhism teaches that envy arises at the very least from attachment to one's dreams, hatred of the achievements of others, and a lack of awareness of the impermanent nature of existence. The Dhammapada, one of the middle texts of Buddhism, gives several teachings about jealousy: "Let jealousy cease, let joy be transcended, let lovers be controlled. In this way, peace will follow."

"He who envies others finds no peace, he who abstains from jealousy has calm thoughts." (Dhammapada, 179)

Buddhism encourages people to develop qualities such as equanimity, compassion, and loving-kindness (metta) to overcome jealousy. The practice of mindfulness helps individuals become aware of their jealous thoughts and feelings, allowing them to address these feelings with awareness and clarity.

**Moral and spiritual consequences of jealousy in Buddhism**

In Buddhism, jealousy has several negative consequences:

**1. Mental anguish:** jealousy creates inner chaos, which gives rise to frustration, anger, and despair.

**2. Attachment to the ego:** jealousy strengthens the ego, which in Buddhist teachings is the primary cause of suffering. It prevents the loss of knowledge about the interconnectedness of all beings and the loss of self.

**3. Obstacle to Enlightenment:** Jealousy, like various mental afflictions, acts as a hindrance to spiritual development. It keeps the character trapped in cycles of attachment and aversion, preventing them from achieving enlightenment. To overcome jealousy, Buddhism encourages mindfulness, meditation, and the cultivation of the Four Noble Truths and the Eightfold Path, which lead to the cessation of struggle and the improvement of inner peace. Jealousy is consistently recognized as a flawed and unfavorable emotion in these diverse religious traditions. Islam, Christianity, Judaism, and Buddhism all teach that jealousy stems from insecurity, attachment, and dissatisfaction with what is. While each way of life offers its own personal direction. Towards overcoming envy—whether through prayer, love, contentment, or mindfulness—one common knowledge may be that envy harms not only the man or woman but also their relationships with others and with the divine.

The moral and spiritual effects of envy—whether they are secular decline, social discord, or mental suffering—illustrate the importance of cultivating virtues such as gratitude, humility, contentment, and compassion. By overcoming envy, individuals can live harmonious, peaceful, and happy lives in harmony with the values of their respective faiths.

# Chapter 6: Jealousy and Society - How This Emotion Destroys Societies.

Jealousy is often dismissed as a private or isolated feeling, something that only affects the man or woman who experiences it. However, this emotion has far-reaching effects beyond the man or woman. It permeates the fabric of society, affecting relationships, families, offices, or even entire communities.

From petty rivalry between friends to harmful behavior in professional settings, jealousy has the power to poison social interactions and undermine collective cohesion. Here, we are able to explore how jealousy damages diverse social structures, as well as the function that cultural norms play in both maintaining and reducing this emotion.

1. **The Social Impact of Jealousy in Relationships, Families, and Workplaces**

   Jealousy in Personal Relationships Jealousy is a leading cause of conflict in private relationships, especially in romantic partnerships. While a certain amount of jealousy can be herbaceous, when it becomes excessive, it can be unusually negative.

   In romantic relationships, jealousy regularly arises when one partner feels threatened by the perceived attention or affection that their partner offers to someone else. This can result in a lack of trust, possessiveness, and emotional manipulation.

   Psychological damage to partners:

   **Erosion of trust:** When jealousy takes hold, it erodes trust between partners. Constant accusations, surveillance, or emotional outbursts create an atmosphere of suspicion.

   Over time, this can leave one or both partners feeling emotionally drained, which can lead to a breakup of the relationship.

**Cycle of insecurity:** For the partner experiencing jealousy, the feelings often stem from a deep-seated lack of trust. This insecurity is then amplified by jealousy, creating a vicious cycle. Instead of addressing the root causes of their fear, people maintain interactions in jealous behaviors, which only harm the relationship.

**Controlling Behavior:** Jealousy can also manifest as controlling behaviors, in which one partner tries to limit the other's interactions with friends, family, or colleagues. This dynamic not only erodes the jealous partner's autonomy but also creates tension and resentment in dating.

**Family Dynamics and Sibling Rivalry:**
**Parental Favoritism:** In families, jealousy often manifests itself between siblings.
Children may also experience jealousy over a sibling's achievements, a parent's interests, or even clothing items.
When parents inadvertently promote competition by showing favoritism, it can deepen these feelings of resentment and divide siblings, leaving long-term emotional scars.

**Insecure parents:** Parents who are themselves insecure or jealous may unknowingly pass these unhealthy traits on to their children. For example, a mother who feels threatened by her daughter's path to glory or fulfillment can also damage the child's self-esteem, causing emotional damage that can be a challenge to control as they mature.

**Generational effects:**
Jealousy in families can be passed down from generation to generation, creating a cycle of emotional damage. Children who grow up in environments where jealousy is high may also struggle with jealousy in their personal relationships and pass this behavior

on to their children. Thus, the emotional costs of jealousy can mount over the years, perpetuating unhealthy dynamics in families. Jealousy within the workplace Jealousy is not limited to non-public relationships. It is also capable of wreaking havoc in professional settings.

In the workplace, jealousy often arises in response to opposition to promotions, fame, or resources. Employees who feel undervalued or underappreciated may also become green with jealousy of their colleagues who receive accolades or opportunity they desire.

**Impact on work culture:** Reduced collaboration: Jealousy can undermine teamwork and collaboration. Employees who are exposed to threats by their peers may be less inclined to share pertinent information, ideas, or support. Instead of working collectively to achieve organizational goals, they may adopt an "I am against them" mentality, focusing more on individual success than the collective well-being of the team.

**Backstabbing and sabotage:** In extreme cases, jealousy in the workplace can result in backstabbing, gossip, and sabotage. An employee who feels that their role is at risk may attempt to undermine the fulfillment of their colleague through malicious gossip or perhaps planned actions intended to discredit them. This creates a toxic work environment where trust is lost and morale is low.

**Burnout and attrition:** In workplaces where jealousy is rife, employees can also experience high levels of stress and burnout.

Those who are the targets of jealousy often find themselves exhausted by the emotional burden they carry to protect their role. This can result in excessive employee turnover, decreased job satisfaction, and decreased overall organizational performance.

Envy in Communities and Society When envy permeates entire groups, it can lead to distrust, division, and resentment. In close-knit communities, envy can manifest itself in the form of social exclusion, gossip, and even violence. Those who experience exclusion or deprivation can also develop envy toward more privileged people, and this can cause collective unrest.

**Social Division and Class Tension**: Economic Inequality: In societies with a sharp division between rich and poor, envy can become a powerful social force. Evil people may envy the wealth and status of the rich, to the point where the rich may look down on the poor, which can lead to anxiety and fighting. In severe cases, this envy can lead to protests, riots, and the breakdown of the social order.

**Social Exclusion:**

In close-knit societies, envy often occurs within the social exclusion of people or companies that are considered "higher status." It may manifest in envy over perceived favoritism due to physical appearance, social where envy is considered a natural response to seeing others succeed.

**Individualism vs. Collectivism:**

In individualistic cultures (e.g., the United States and Western Europe), people are often encouraged to compete for personal fulfillment and recognition. This fosters an environment in which envy is more likely to arise, especially when someone feels that a colleague, friend, or family member threatens his or her personal success.

On the other hand, collectivist cultures (e.g., many Asian and African cultures) emphasize group cohesion and cooperation, which can reduce feelings of envy by promoting harmony and the experience of shared success.

**Cultural celebrations of success:** In cultures where success is seen as the ultimate measure of good worth—whether or not in terms of wealth, prestige, or power—envy becomes more prominent. The idea that only a few can succeed leads people to view the accomplishments of others as opportunities for their own potential, rather than as opportunities for shared happiness and growth.

Envy is not just a private emotion—it has profound effects on relationships, families, workplaces, and society as a whole. This emotion can break trust, create divisions, and perpetuate negative cycles of resentment and opposition. In the business world, envy undermines teamwork and cooperation, while in families; it fosters competition and squelches deliberation.

In communities, envy can cause social unrest, cultural divisions, or even violence.

Cultural influences also play a large role in increasing or decreasing envy.

While some cultures normalize envy through media portrayals or social expectations, others may also foster a more communal attitude that prioritizes cooperation over opposition.

The key to overcoming envy on a social level lies in fostering values such as empathy.

Gratitude, and collective kindness, rather than comparisons and comparisons between men or women. As we move through the next chapter, we will explore the mental mechanisms behind jealousy, analyzing the triggers and underlying fears that power this emotion and the ways we deal with it, both individually and collectively.

## Chapter 7: The Jealous Mindset –
### How to Recognize the Signs of Jealousy:
**Jealousy is a deeply rooted and often unconscious emotion.**
Unlike more obvious fearful feelings like anger or sadness, jealousy tends to work quietly beneath the surface, manifesting itself in a regular, diffuse manner. This makes it difficult for many people to understand jealousy in them or in others. In relationships, workplaces, and social interactions, jealousy can lead to misunderstandings, resentment, and conflict. That is why it is important to recognize the signs early. Here, we will explore how jealousy manifests itself.
In ourselves and in others. We will look at common attitudes and perceptions towards jealousy and offer insightful insights into how to identify this emotion

before it gets out of hand. Recognizing jealousy is the first step towards dealing with it and reducing its negative impact on our lives and relationships.

1.Identifying Jealousy in Yourself It is often difficult to detect jealousy within yourself, as it disguises itself as feelings of insecurity, frustration, or resentment. However, positive internal cues and perception patterns can serve as signs that jealousy is at play.

Physical Symptoms of Jealousy Our feelings often manifest physically, and jealousy is no exception. When we feel jealous, we experience physical symptoms that signal an internal emotional disturbance:

Tightness in the chest or a heavy feeling inside the stomach. Rapid heartbeat or a feeling of restlessness. Anxiousness or the urge to behave unexpectedly (for example, sending an accusatory message or confronting the man or woman involved). Sweating or feeling excessively hot in situations that provoke jealousy. These physical symptoms are usually associated with the frame's stress response. Feelings of jealousy can trigger the release of stress hormones like cortisol, which triggers a "fight or flight" response, which culminates in the aforementioned physical symptoms.

Emotional and Cognitive Indicators Jealousy often emerges from a combination of lack of confidence, fear, and self-doubt. If you notice these emotional patterns, jealousy may be at its root:

**Insecurity**: A persistent feeling of inadequacy, fear of being left behind, or trauma that others are more capable or deserving. Fear of loss: When you feel threatened by someone else's presence, achievements, or interest that diminishes your personal worth or popularity.

**Comparing yourself to others:** A pervasive addiction to measuring your worth against the achievements, possessions, or attributes of others. This conflict often ends in feelings of jealousy when it seems like someone else has more or is being praised than you.
**A jealous mind might think**: "Why do they always get what I want?"
"I'm not good enough for them anymore."
"Why do people like them more than me?" "I'm afraid they'll take what I have."
If you find that your mind is constantly spinning, jealousy can affect your thinking and behavior.
**Internal Conflict and Self-**Talk A jealous mindset can often be related to unhealthy internal dialogue. For example, when someone else gets something you want, you are likely to say to yourself:
"They don't deserve it."
"I should have had it instead."
"I've worked harder; why haven't I gotten this much popularity?"
This self-talk often ends in feelings of bitterness, resentment, and even anger.
In some instances, jealousy can lead to self-sabotage, where you undermine your own happiness in an attempt to justify your jealousy. The need to compete Jealousy regularly pushes humans into dangerous confrontations.
If you find yourself constantly trying to outdo others, this could be a sign of jealousy. Instead of celebrating the successes of others, you may feel the need to prove that you are superior or more deserving.
2. Identifying Jealousy in Others While it can be difficult to recognize jealousy in yourself, it can be much easier to be aware of it in others. Often, we can see jealousy in the attitudes and behaviors of those around us.

Below are common signs that someone may be experiencing jealousy.

### . Passive-aggressive Behavior

One of the most common signs of jealousy in others is passive-aggressive behavior.

A jealous man or woman will not brazenly express their feelings.

However, they will express their displeasure in indirect ways, including: Backhanded compliments: "Wow, that get-up dressing is first-class. I could never pull something like that off for myself; however, it really works for you."

### Sarcasm or cutting remarks:

These comments are often disguised as jokes but have an underlying sting that reveals jealousy or a lack of confidence. Subtle harm: They may be little your achievements or diminish your accomplishments in an attempt to diminish your perceived value.

2. Gossiping or spreading rumors jealous people regularly resort to gossiping or spreading rumors to undermine those they feel threatened by.
3. If you know, someone is constantly talking behind your back. The backlash of another man or woman—especially someone they may feel resentment toward—may be a sign that jealousy is at play. Gossip is often intended to tarnish the reputation or accomplishments of the alternative character, thus enhancing the jealous man or woman's experience of superiority.
4. Emotional withdrawal or distancing can sometimes be a feature of jealous people. They withdraw emotionally or stop interacting as much as possible with the character they feel threatened by. This can happen in both non-public and professional relationships.

For example, a colleague may start talking to you or distance him or herself when you receive a promotion or recognition. Jealousy manifests itself as passive resistance to your success.

5. Overly critical or judgmental another sign of jealousy in others is an overly critical mindset.

A jealous person will often find fault with everything you do, no matter how small. They may criticize your achievements, your appearance, or your personality—anything that makes you feels inferior or undeserving of yourself. They may also focus on small flaws to lower your self-esteem and diminish your success.

5. Competition and One-Up Man ship If someone constantly competes with you, even in situations where there is no real need for competition, they are probably jealous.

For example, they may always try to "outdo" you by doing more work, acquiring more material possessions, or demonstrating superior knowledge. This is often a sign of an underlying jealousy that stems from insecurity.

6. In addition to being overly complimentary or giving false praise, some jealous people may additionally compliment someone in a way that feels disrespectful. Their flattery may be excessive or appear forced, and it can often feel like a cover for manipulation or creating an artificial sense of goodwill. They may also praise you just enough to appear supportive, while hiding their own legitimate feelings of jealousy.

## 3. Common Behavioral and Thinking Patterns of Jealous People.

Jealous people often exhibit certain cognitive styles and behavioral tendencies that help them to understand this emotion more clearly. Recognizing these patterns can provide insight into both private and interpersonal struggles with jealousy.

1. Preoccupation with Others' Success Jealous people regularly becomes deeply preoccupied with the achievements or assets of others. They may spend all their time mastering what other people have—whether it's material wealth, romantic relationships, social fame, or professional achievements—and evaluating it in terms of their own personal circumstances. Their thoughts may constantly wander downward toward perceived disparities. "Why do they usually appreciate my equals?"
"Why does everyone love them more than me?"
This regular evaluation can make them feel unworthy or green with envy, specializing in the perceived flaws of their own personal lifestyles rather than appreciating what they already have.

2. **Fear of Loss or Rejection**
Jealous people often worry deeply about losing something or someone they value, whether it is a romantic partner, a friendship, or a career opportunity. This fear leads them to constantly screen and scrutinize the actions of others, especially those they perceive as competition.
"I want to make sure no one gets too close to my partner."
"I can't let my partner get ahead of me in front of the boss."

3. **Desire to Control Others**
A jealous man or woman may additionally try to control or manipulate those them are green with jealousy towards. For example, a jealous friend may try to manipulate where you are going or whom you are unquestionably seeing because they are afraid that someone else will take your interest away from them. Similarly, a jealous partner may limit your interactions with others to prevent you

from forming close relationships with people they feel threatened by.

4. **Lack of empathy**

    Jealous people often struggle to feel overtly happy about others' successes. Instead of celebrating someone else's success, they feel envious or bitter. They may hide behind a fake display of happiness. However, deep down, they feel green with envy and are self-conscious about their own personal shortcomings.

This lack of empathy is a trademark of jealousy, as it prevents them from acknowledging and celebrating others' successes, as they should. Recognizing jealousy — whether in they or in others — is the first step toward managing and overcoming this unpleasant emotion.

By paying attention to the physical, emotional, and behavioral signs and symptoms of jealousy, we can increase our awareness of its effects and take steps to deal with it.

For people, self-awareness is essential to breaking the cycle of jealousy, while for those who see jealousy in others, empathy and open communication can help address the underlying insecurities and reduce the negative consequences of jealousy.

As we move through the next chapter, we are able to discover sensible techniques for overcoming jealousy and developing a fit mindset.

One that embraces self-esteem, gratitude, and contentment, both personally and within our relationships.

## Chapter 8: Jealousy and Relationships—
**How It Destroys Love and Trust.**

Jealousy is a powerful and damaging emotion that can undermine the foundation of any relationship, whether romantic, familial, or platonic. While some stages of jealousy may seem harmless or perhaps normal, when it becomes pervasive or unchecked, it can distort judgment, create resentment, and ultimately destroy a relationship. In romantic partnerships, jealousy can manifest as a lack of trust, possessiveness, or controlling behavior, leading to emotional or even physical distance between partners.

In friendships and family dynamics, jealousy can create divisions that break bonds and create lasting emotional scars.

### 1. Corrosive Effects of Jealousy on Romantic Relationships

Romantic relationships are primarily responsible for the toxic consequences of jealousy. When partners feel jealous, it can create feelings of inadequacy, distrust, and abandonment concerns.

Jealousy often stems from insecurity and fear of losing the other man or woman to someone or something else, which can lead to possessiveness and controlling behavior. Over time, this creates a toxic cycle that destroys a lot of consideration and intimacy, which can be important for healthy dating. Jealousy in Romantic Relationships

**Roots Insecurity and Low Self-Esteem:**
Often, jealousy stems from a deep-seated experience of personal insecurity or low self-esteem. One partner may also perceive that they are no longer
"Good enough"
For the other, leading them to worry that someone more attractive, exciting, or accomplished will come along and take over. This worry of inadequacy manifests itself in Jealousy, which can also lead to possessiveness and attempts to control the relationship.

**Fear of abandonment:** For many people, jealousy is linked to a deep fear of abandonment or betrayal. If a partner feels their significant other is listening to someone else, it can trigger an underlying fear of their own abandonment. This fear often fuels jealousy, which can make a person overreact to perceived threats to the connection, even if no real threat exists.

**Past trauma or insecurity:**
Previous experiences of betrayal, infidelity, or abandonment can increase someone's tendency to become jealous. If a person has been cheated on in the past, they will carry the wounds into future relationships, making them hypersensitive to any scenario that could be interpreted as an opportunity for potential.

How Jealousy Destroys Trust in Romantic Relationships. Trust is the foundation of any strong relationship, and jealousy is one of the most common destroyers.

Belief When jealousy becomes common or extreme, it creates a climate of suspicion and insecurity that undermines open communication and mutual knowledge. Here are some ways jealousy damages:

**Accusations and False Suspicions**

A jealous partner may begin to accuse his or her well-meaning partner of factors that are not happening—such as infidelity or flirting with someone else. These accusations may be based on nothing more than a distorted perception of imagined events or activities. Over time, these unfounded accusations erode trust and cause each partner to feel emotionally insecure.

**Controlling Behavior:** Jealousy can lead to a controlling partner, seeking to limit the other person's freedom or interactions with others. This may include setting rules about who the partner can talk to, what they can do, or how they spend their time. While these behaviors may be considered connection protecting, they can actually drive each partner apart in the end, leaving one feeling trapped and the other feeling overwhelmed.

**Emotional Distance:** In many cases, jealousy results in emotional withdrawal. When a partner becomes jealous, they withdraw from their partner or respond with coldness, anger, or silence.

This emotional distance destroys intimacy and creates a gap between partners, as well as increasing insecurity and jealousy.

**Possessiveness and Control:**

A Cycle of Destruction Possessiveness is usually a manifestation of jealousy. When one partner feels overly possessive, they may try to control their partner's interactions, play, or friendships. This possessiveness comes from an area of fear—the fear of losing the other person's collaborate, the fear of being replaced, or the fear of rejection. Over time, possessive behaviors can emerge as suffocating and disruptive to the connection.

**Isolating from Others:**
A possessive partner may try to isolate the opposing partner from friends, family, or the partner regularly under the guise of "protecting" the connection. This isolating behavior no longer takes away the partner's freedom but rather breeds resentment and fighting.

**Monitoring or Checking:**
In many cases, jealousy manifests itself as constant checking of a partner's whereabouts, messages, or social media activities.

This behavior often known as "cyber squatting" or "checking in," is an attempt to control or monitor a partner's movements and reinforce feelings of dominance.

While it may offer temporary reassurance, it destroys trust in the end and creates a toxic ecosystem.

5. **Navigating Jealousy in Friendships** While jealousy is regularly associated with romantic relationships, it can also be a major challenge in friendships. Friendships are built on trust and mutual admiration, and jealousy can quickly undermine both of these pillars. Jealousy in friendships regularly arises while one friend perceives their replacement as additional attention, love, or fulfillment, leading to feelings of conflict and resentment.

**Signs of Jealousy in Friendships Competition for Attention:**
A jealous friend may also compete for attention, whether it is from mutual friends, romantic partners, or other humans in the friend group. They may subtly (or no longer so subtly) try to bring you down or make you feel inferior in order to gain validation or approval.

**Gossiping or talking behind your back:**

Jealous friends may also gossip about you or undermine your achievements in front of others. Instead of celebrating your success, they may belittle your appearance or spread rumors to make you look terrible, often as a way to deal with their own insecurities or feelings of jealousy.

**Withdrawing or passive-aggressive behavior:**
A jealous friend may ignore your achievements or harshly criticize your choices, as well as emotionally withdraw from you or communicate in a passive-competitive manner.

Their jealousy can also take the form of resentment, making it difficult to maintain a balanced and trusting friendship. How jealousy damages friendships.

**Erosion of trust:**
Just as jealousy destroys rapport in romantic relationships, it has the power to undermine friendships.

When a chum acts out of jealousy, it can make the other person feel unsupported or betrayed. Jealous behaviors such as gossiping or belittling can cause feelings of distrust, which can be difficult to repair.

**Competition instead of support:**
Ideally, friendships are built on mutual support and knowledge. However, jealousy often turns friendships into competitions.

A jealous friend may also make fun of your success because they may be preoccupied with their own perceived shortcomings or a desire to outdo you. Instead of being a source of encouragement, jealousy turns friendships into a battleground for justification.

**Damage to the emotional connection**:

Jealousy can poison the emotional bond that friends share. If a friend constantly feels threatened by your achievements or relationships, it can create a rift between you. Over time, this emotional disconnect weakens the bond, making it difficult to maintain a healthy and happy friendship.

**Navigating Jealousy in Friendships Open Communication:**

The key to navigating jealousy in friendships is open, honest verbal exchanges. If you sense that a chum is acting out of jealousy, addressing it immediately can prevent misunderstandings. It's crucial to create an area where both friends feel safe sharing their feelings and concerns.

**Celebrate Each Other's Successes:**

A healthy friendship thrives on mutual support. Celebrating each other's successes and lifting each other up is a powerful antidote to jealousy. Recognizing that one friend's success does not diminish the value of the other can help reduce feelings of competition and foster an environment of trust and cooperation.

6. **Jealousy in Family Dynamics**

Family relationships can be fundamentally complicated when jealousy comes into play. Jealousy between siblings, parents, or extended family members can cause lifelong tension and division. While sibling rivalry is a common example, jealousy can also manifest when one family member feels neglected, unimportant, or ignored in favor of others.

**Jealousy between siblings**:

One of the most common and uncommon triggers for sibling jealousy is thought to be favoritism on the part of parents. A sibling who feels they are constantly not noticed or are being treated unfairly may also develop resentment and jealousy toward the popular sibling.

This jealousy can lead to competition, arguments, and strained family dynamics.

**Attention and resources:**

As children develop, they may experience jealousy over shared assets such as interests, affection, or fabric goods. A man or woman's desire for popularity can fuel rivalry, creating friction between siblings that can persist into adulthood.

**Jealousy between parents and children**

**Parental rivalry**:

In some cases, jealousy can arise between fathers, mothers, and their children, especially when children surpass their parents in certain areas, including academic or professional achievements. Parents may also feel threatened by their youngster's achievements, which can lead to jealousy and subtle vulnerability.

**Jealousy over parental attention:**

Children, especially young children, may experience jealousy when they perceive that a sibling is receiving extra attention or affection from a certain person. This is often seen in two-child households, where opposition to parental love can lead to jealousy and a lack of trust. Jealousy can be an insidious pressure that destroys the music of love, along with acceptance of the truth, and emotional connection in romantic relationships, friendships, and family dynamics. While jealousy is a natural human emotion, when left unchecked it can cause profound harm, eroding the bonds that collectively hold relationships together.

Recognizing the signs and symptoms of jealousy in yourself and others is the first step to reducing its impact. By engaging in open verbal exchanges, cultivating empathy, and cultivating self-awareness, it is far more feasible to navigate jealousy and build stronger, more trusting relationships.

As we move through the next chapter, we can explore practical techniques for overcoming jealousy, offering support to individuals and couples to rebuild trust, and moving forward with healthier ideas about love, competition, and personal growth.

## Chapter 9: The Impact of Jealousy on Health –

The Mind-Body Connection Jealousy is not just an emotion that affects our relationships; it also has profound physical and mental consequences that can harm our overall health. While many people think of jealousy as a simple emotional response, studies show that it can trigger a cascade of physiological responses within the frame, leading to increased stress, anxiety, and even depression. Thoughts and frames are deeply intertwined, and unhealthy emotions like jealousy can have a profound impact on both. In this chapter, we can explore how jealousy manifests itself physically, the ways it affects the frame, and the mental health struggles that can arise as a result.

By understanding the mind-body connection of jealousy, we can begin to recognize the broader health implications of this emotion and take steps to address it before it escalates into additional fitness issues.

1. How jealousy manifests itself physically. When we experience jealousy, the brain interprets it as a threat, which sets off a cascade of physical responses. Jealousy activates the same neural pathways that might be activated in moments of fear, frustration, or anger.

    This culminates in the release of either stress hormones like cortical and adrenaline, which prepare the body to "fight" or "flight" from danger.

    However, unlike more external threats, the occasion caused by jealousy is regularly internal and emotional, making it difficult to control the physical response.

    The fight-or-flight response the "fight-or-flight" response, a physical response to a perceived threat, is triggered by jealousy in a frighteningly similar way to other intense emotions. The frame is primed for action by the release of the following hormones:

**Cortisol:**
Known as the "stress hormone," cortisol is released during moments of stress and prepares the body to deal with the situation. It increases heart rate, increases blood pressure, and directs more blood to the muscles, preparing them for short-term physical activity.

**Adrenaline (Epinephrine):**
Adrenaline, the hormone responsible for the fight-or-flight response, is released during moments of great anxiety or distress. It causes the body to become extra alert, with symptoms including a rapid heartbeat, dry mouth, rapid breathing, and trembling.

These physical responses, while beneficial in the immediate term in the event of a real situation, can be dangerous if the perceived "threat" is psychological and ongoing, as in the case of jealousy. When jealousy becomes persistent, these stress responses can wreak havoc on the frame.

**Physical Symptoms of Jealousy**
Jealousy can cause a variety of physical signs and symptoms, many of which are related to the body's stress response.

**These may include:**
Increased heart rate or palpitations Shallow breathing or hyperventilation Muscle tension, especially in the shoulders, neck, and back Digestive problems, including nausea, stomach pain, or indigestion. Headaches or

migraines Sweating, especially in situations where jealousy is triggered Dry mouth, which can make it difficult to really talk or communicate These physical symptoms are often more commonly reported in moments of extreme jealousy, including when a person feels the potential threat of being ignored in their relationship or in favor of someone else.

2. **The Link between Jealousy and Stress**

Chronic jealousy, especially if it is not addressed now, can turn into chronic stress. When jealousy is a common emotional experience, it causes the frame to be overly alert, creating constant stress and tension. Chronic activation of the stress response occurs when jealousy is repeatedly skilled or altered. Chronic, it affects the continuous activation of the frame's stress response. This prolonged activation has a number of terrible effects on the body,

Including:

**Weakened immune system**:

Chronic stress suppresses the immune system, making people more vulnerable to illnesses such as colds, infections, and various fitness problems. The frame's ability to fight infection is reduced, leading to a general decline in physical health.

**High blood pressure:**

Prolonged onset of cortisol and adrenaline can increase blood pressure, which can increase the risk of cardiovascular problems such as high blood pressure, heart disease, and stroke.

**Sleep disturbances:** Chronic jealousy and stress can interfere with sleep patterns, making it difficult to fall asleep, stay asleep, or get a restful night's sleep. This can cause insomnia, fatigue, and a predominance of physical and mental exhaustion.

**Muscle tension and pain:**
The anxiety associated with jealousy often manifests itself physically in the form of tight muscles, especially in the neck, shoulders, and back. Over time, this can lead to ongoing pain, complications, or anxiety-related issues, including temporomandibular joint (TMJ) disease. Emotional stress and its long-term effects Jealousy is not an emotional strain that will go away once the situation is resolved. When jealousy becomes chronic, it has long-term mental consequences, leading to increased symptoms of stress and depression. This is partly because jealousy is often fueled by feelings of inadequacy, loss, and insecurity. It can hold the frame and mind in a constant state of emotional suffering.

Over time, these emotional scars can lead to burnout, exhaustion, and a diminished ability to cope with the pressures of life. The constant emotional turmoil that results from jealousy can also make it difficult for people to feel emotionally secure in their relationships, leading to further distress.

2. **Mental Health Consequences of Jealousy**
While the physical consequences of jealousy are great, its psychological and emotional toll can be just as negative. Chronic jealousy can lead to anxiety, depression, and a damaged sense of self-esteem, as well as serious mental health problems. These mental health problems are linked to the way the frame responds to jealousy, and they often feed off

each other in a vicious cycle. Jealousy and Anxiety is not an uncommon consequence of persistent jealousy. When jealousy is generalized or turns into a pervasive emotional pleasure, it creates a constant reign of worry and anxiety.

People who enjoy jealousy may also experience that they are constantly on edge, waiting for something to "go wrong" in their relationships or personal lives. This heightened experience of alertness, aided by anxiety, regularly triggers feelings of fear, anxiety, and irritability.

**Hyper vigilance:**
People who are jealous are often hyper vigilant, constantly scanning their environment for signs of perceived threats. In romantic relationships, for example, this may mean obsessively checking your partner's phone or social media profiles for evidence of infidelity or infidelity.

**Paranoia:** The anxiety associated with jealousy can lead to feelings of paranoia. People who feel jealous may also believe that others are conspiring against them or that their fears of being changed or abandoned are valid, even when there is no solid evidence. Jealousy and depression Envy is also associated with sadness, especially when it stems from feelings of inadequacy or hopelessness. Individuals who suffer from persistent jealousy often feel unworthy or inferior to those they envy. Over time, these feelings of self-doubt can deepen, leading to despair.

**Low self-esteem:**

Jealousy is often caused by low self-esteem, and over time, it can erode a person's confidence in their abilities, appearance, or relationships. This constant self-criticism can result in negative thinking patterns and feelings of purposelessness.

**Loss of motivation:**
Depression because of jealousy can make it difficult for people to achieve their dreams or the sense of inspiration they need to improve their lives. They may also become inactive, withdrawing from activities that bring them joy, and instead focusing on what others have or are achieving. **Social isolation:**
As jealousy and depression increase, people may begin to withdraw from social interactions. They may become emotionally withdrawn or feel ashamed of their jealous feelings, which can result in isolation from friends, family, and loved ones.

The cycle of jealousy, anxiety, and depression
Jealousy, anxiety, and frustration can create a vicious cycle.

The more jealous someone feels, the busier they are, and the greater the risk of frustration. This cycle can be self-inflicted, making it harder for the character to block out the weak emotions.

As the character becomes more isolated and consumed by these emotions, their mental well-being continues to deteriorate, in addition to the effects of jealousy increasing.

3. **Breaking the Cycle:**
Addressing the Physical and Mental Effects of Jealousy Understanding the connection between mindset and the impact of jealousy

on well-being is important for figuring out ways to disrupt the cycle. Some strategies for dealing with the physical and mental well-being consequences of jealousy are:

**1. Mindfulness and stress reduction techniques.**

Mindfulness and relaxation strategies can help reduce the physical symptoms of jealousy by helping to calm the body's stress response. Exercises including deep breathing, meditation, and yoga can reduce cortisol and adrenaline levels within the frame, which helps relieve stress and muscle tension.

**5. Cognitive Behavioral Therapy (CBT)**

CBT is a powerful healing technique that can help people overcome jealousy by becoming aware of negative thought patterns. By challenging the irrational beliefs and assumptions that fuel jealousy, CBT helps people reframe their perceptions and expand healthier ways of wondering.

4. **Improving Self-Esteem**

Since jealousy is often rooted in a lack of trust and self-esteem, creating a sense of urgency is an important step in overcoming it. Engaging in self-compassion, practicing gratitude, and dreaming privately can help improve self-esteem and reduce the likelihood of feeling jealous.

4. Open Communication in Relationships In romantic relationships, open communication is key to dealing with jealousy. Partners can express their insecurities and fears in a safe, nonjudgmental way that minimizes misunderstandings and provides constructive

consideration. When jealousy arises, actively discussing feelings can prevent them from escalating and damaging the connection. Jealousy is not only an emotional and relational challenge, but it also has profound effects on our physical and mental health. Chronic jealousy results in stress, tension, and sadness, which affect the frame and mind. By recognizing the symptoms of jealousy and its physical manifestations, we can take steps to break the cycle and protect our fitness. Through mindfulness, therapy, open communication, and a focus on building self-esteem, we are able to address the root causes of jealousy and regain a sense of peace and balance in our lives.

## Chapter 10: Is Jealousy a Habit of Unsuccessful People?

The Connection between Envy and Personal Stagnation How Envy Undermines Growth and Success Envy is often considered a toxic emotion, one that poisons relationships, clouds judgment, and inhibits emotional well-being. However, is envy simply a natural human response to jealousy, or does it serves as a symptom of deeper, more personal issues? Many people experience joy in moments of envy, but some people hold onto it as a permanent emotional burden, allowing it to dictate their actions and minds. Over time, this emotion can emerge as a powerful force that undermines their ability to develop, prevail, and achieve their personal and professional goals. Here, we explore the notion that envy can be a coping mechanism for unsuccessful people and observe how envy is linked to personal stagnation. We will examine how envy can sabotage growth, prevent personal growth, and keep people from realizing their true potential. Furthermore, we will analyze how envy works against success, in terms of each attitude and behavior, and present a concept for how it can be overcome.

1. **The Link Between Envy and Personal Stagnation**

    Success is often defined by the ability to set dreams, work hard towards achieving them, and overcome limitations along the way. However, envy, with its deep roots in evaluation, lack of confidence, and fear of loss, works quickly towards this mindset of acceleration and growth. People who suffer from constant envy often find themselves trapped in a cycle of resentment and self-doubt, which limits their potential and prevents them from moving forward.

    **The Comparison Trap:** Envy as an Obstacle to Progress Envy is a key way to undermine personal fulfillment by trapping people in a cycle of constant contradiction. When a person is jealous of the successes of others, they often spend more time mastering what others have or are lacking than developing their own. These evaluation-based questions lead to dissatisfaction and self-complaining, each of which can be destructive to non-public development.

**Negative self-talk:** Jealous people often criticize themselves for not being able to achieve what others have. This terrible self-talk reinforces feelings of inadequacy, creating a barrier to fulfillment. Instead of using the successes of others as motivation, the jealous man or woman may additionally feel inferior or unworthy, preventing them from achieving and pursuing their dreams.

**Lack of motivation:** Constantly measuring themselves against others can lead to a lack of motivation. Instead of being motivated by the success of another person, the jealous man or woman feels threatened by it. This worry of being left behind or ignored makes it difficult for them to focus on their own direction, which leads to stagnation.

**Overemphasis on external validation:** Jealousy is often fueled by a need for external validation. People who are jealous may also measure their true worth by the way they evaluate others, rather than developing an internal sense of worth. As a result, they are more likely to seek approval or attention from others rather than develop the internal self-confidence needed for personal success.

**Fear of Failure:**

Its Role in Jealousy and Risk Avoidance
Envy is often rooted in a fear of failure. When a person is jealous of another person's success, it is often rooted in the belief that they are somehow "less than" or incapable of reaching parity. This belief can lead to avoidant behaviors, such as procrastination, self-doubt, and unwillingness to take risks.

**Fear of Action:**
People who suffer from envy may also experience paralysis from the fear of failure. They see others achieving success and believe that they cannot measure up in any way. This mindset discourages them from taking active steps toward their goals because they are too afraid of failing.

**Perfectionism:**
Envy can also fuel perfectionist tendencies. Choosing to conform to or surpass another person can cause a jealous person to give up until they feel that everything is "perfect." This stalling behavior, driven by a fear of imperfection, often leads to stagnation and loss of real growth.

2. **How Jealousy Hurts Growth and Success**
The psychology of jealousy is closely linked to personal growth and success. When jealousy is allowed to flourish unchecked, it has the potential to actively hinder growth, especially by fostering an unhealthy mindset and limiting the ability to take positive action.

3. **Jealousy breeds negative emotions and reduces productivity.**

When we are caught in the grip of jealousy, we experience a range of frightening feelings that sap our mental energy and interest. Time and energy that could be spent on effective tasks are instead consumed by rumination, resentment, and frustration. This emotional drain reduces productivity, making it difficult to focus on tasks that contribute to non-public and professional fulfillment.

**Loss of attention:**

Jealousy takes our attention away from our own desires and focuses it on someone else's existence or achievements. Instead of focusing on our own personal goals, we become excited about what others are doing. This misdirected energy not only wastes time but also reduces our ability to accomplish meaningful tasks. Increased stress and burnout: Jealousy can also lead to chronic stress because it often stems from a lack of confidence or a fear of not measuring up. This emotional and intellectual strain can result in burnout, making it difficult to maintain a focus and make significant efforts toward long-term fulfillment.

**Negative emotional states:**

Jealousy can lead to feelings of bitterness, resentment, anger, and frustration. These feelings sap our ability to feel gratitude and joy, which are key components of maintaining a high-quality mindset and staying motivated. When negative feelings take over, it becomes difficult to maintain the emotional resilience necessary for success.

## 2. Jealousy destroys relationships and networking opportunities.

Success often depends on the relationships we form—whether in private networks, professional circles, or groups of like-minded individuals. Jealousy can damage these relationships by increasing hostility, bitterness, and distrust. When a person is constantly resentful of others, it becomes difficult to build genuine, collaborative relationships based on mutual respect and recognition.

**Damage to professional relationships:**
In the management arena, jealousy can create a hostile competitive environment. Instead of viewing colleagues as allies of competence, the jealous individual may see them as adversaries. This mindset can lead to loss of cooperation, poor teamwork, and missed opportunities for growth or advancement.

**Isolation and disconnection:**
Jealousy can also result in social isolation. When a person is consumed by jealousy, they often withdraw from social interactions or sabotage relationships. This isolation limits the opportunities for non-public and professional growth that come from networking, learning from others, and sharing assets.

**Toxic Behavior and Gossip:**

Envious people may also engage in gossip or demeaning behavior, attempting to discredit those they envy, or creating divisions in social circles. Such toxic behavior not only damages a person's relationships but also creates an environment of distrust and hostility that repels others, making it difficult to form the support networks they seek to achieve.

**3. Envy diverts energy from personal growth.**

Personal growth demands a focal point on self-improvement, study, and developing new abilities. Envy, then, often ends up focusing on what others have done rather than on nurturing their own personal talents or abilities.

**Failure to Learn from Others:**

When a person is jealous of another man or woman, they often fail to see that person's achievements as opportunities for skill and imagination. Instead, jealousy distorts their behavior, causing them to see the other person as a competitor or threat. As a result, they miss valuable guidance that would help them improve themselves.

**Stagnation in Skills and Abilities:**

Instead of pushing themselves to expand and enhance their talent set, jealous people may also fall into a pattern of comparing themselves to others. Instead of taking bold steps to improve, they will remain stuck in their own modern realm, feeling defeated and unable to overcome their obstacles.

**Limited Self-Reflection**

Personal growth requires self-awareness and self-awareness. However, jealousy often blocks this pattern. Instead of examining their own behavior and thought patterns to see how they can improve, a jealous man or woman may spend all their time focusing on the flaws or perceived shortcomings of others. This prevents them from engaging in the kind of constructive self-image that leads to growth.

4. **Breaking the Cycle of Jealousy and Achieving Success**

    Overcoming jealousy is essential to achieving success and reaching your full potential. The first step toward breaking the cycle of jealousy is recognizing its impact on personal and professional growth. By replacing jealousy with positive, growth-oriented behaviors, individuals can open the door to greater success and a happier life.

    1. **Embrace a growth mindset.**

        A growth mindset is the belief that intelligence, abilities, and skills can be developed over years of effort and knowledge. When people adopt a growth mindset, they are less likely to feel threatened by the successes of others. Instead of seeing the successes of others as a source of envy, they see them as an opportunity to gain knowledge and inspiration. **Celebrate the successes of others:** People with a progressive attitude can rejoice in the successes of others without feeling jealous. They understand that another person's success no longer diminishes their own potential. They use the success of others as motivation to keep working towards their dreams. Focus on self-improvement: Instead of judging themselves in front of others, people with a growth mindset are more aware of their own self-improvement. They set personal goals, seek feedback, and frame challenging situations as opportunities to grow and learn.

2. **Practice gratitude:**
   Gratitude is a powerful antidote to envy. When we focus on what we are grateful for in our lives, we begin to shift our mindset from scarcity to abundance. Gratitude helps us appreciate our true adventures, our achievements, and the benefits we have received, which reduces the desire to judge ourselves in front of others.

3. Set clear, achievable goals. Envy often arises when we experience aimlessness or uncertainty about our future. Clear, actionable dreams give us a sense of direction and purpose, which helps quiet the negative mind that is panting with envy. By working toward concrete dreams, we recognize our energy in our own fulfillment in what others are achieving.

Envy is a negative emotion that can hold people back from achieving their full potential. By fostering comparison, insecurity, and fear, envy can undermine personal growth, damage relationships, and reduce productivity. While envy is a natural human emotion, allowing it to dominate our minds and behaviors can lead to stagnation and failure. Success demands a mindset of growth, self-improvement, and resilience. By overcoming envy and mastering our own adventures, we will cultivate the mindset and behavior that culminate in success. In the next chapter, we will examine sensible steps to overcome envy and build the mental and emotional strength needed to achieve lasting success.

## Chapter 11: The Role of Comparison in Envy:

Why We Can't Stop Competing Unaware of the Principle of Social Incongruity and the Need to Break the Trap of Envy

Competing with Others At the heart of envy is a pervasive tendency to compare ourselves to others. Whether in our careers, relationships, appearance, or material fulfillment, humans are clearly wired to conform their lives to the lives of others. This evaluation drives much of the envy we enjoy, increasing our experience of inadequacy, resentment, and insecurity. However, why is evaluation so ingrained in human behavior? In addition, why do we find it so difficult to stop competing with others? In this chapter, we can examine the psychology of the concept of social evaluation and its profound role in fueling envy. We will see how evaluation becomes a temptation that limits our personal growth and happiness and offer techniques for breaking free from its constant cycle. By learning the deeper mechanisms behind social comparison, we can begin to break the vicious patterns of envy and adopt a healthier, more fulfilling approach to our lives and relationships.

1. Social Comparison Theory and the Envy Trap First introduced in 1954 by psychologist Leon Festinger, the social comparison theory states that people have a natural tendency to judge themselves when it comes to others' achievements, and standing. While social comparison can provide useful data for self-evaluation, it can also result in feelings of envy. Inferiority is when we perceive others as superior to us. Upward vs. Downward Comparison a key principle in the idea of social comparison is the distinction between upward and downward comparison. Both types of comparisons do a great job of shaping how we perceive ourselves and the world around us. **Upward Comparison:** It occurs when we compare ourselves to others who are considered superior to us in some way—whether through additional success, beauty, intelligence, or social status. Upward evaluation is a primary driving

force behind envy. When we constantly compare ourselves to those we consider "better," we are likely to feel inferior, envious, and jealous. This increases feelings of envy.

**The Envy Trap**: Envy becomes a common emotional response when we engage in upward evaluation. It is easy to observe another person's accomplishments, relationships, or lifestyle and experience, even though we are losing out in the competition. The more we become aware of the successes of others, the more we reinforce the idea that our own efforts are inadequate or incompetent. This constant evaluation of our lives in opposition to others leads to frustration, self-doubt, and resentment. **Downward comparison**: In evaluation, downward comparison occurs when we compare ourselves to those we consider worse off or much less successful than ourselves. While it may briefly boost our self-esteem, it can also foster arrogance, complacency, or a false sense of superiority. While downward incongruence does not immediately lead to jealousy, it can lead to feelings of complacency or an inflatedsense of self-worth that stunts growth.

**The Constant Need for Validation**

One reason validation is so powerful is that it satisfies an emotional need for validation. When we test ourselves in front of others, we are seeking reassurance about our persona lwel lb eingandability. This validation often comes in the form of social credibility, whether through praise, rewards, or the praise of others.

**Social media and comparison amplifiers:** In the digital age, social incongruence has become even more pervasive, especially through social media. Platforms like Instagram, Facebook, and TikTok gift curated, idealized variations of human lives, making it easier than ever to communicate upward incongruence. People often overextend their accomplishments, vacations, and relationships, which can create feelings of inadequacy in others who are scrolling through their feeds. "Highlight Reel"

**Syndrome:** Social media feeds are essentially spotlight reels that show the best of a person's first-rate moments. This creates the illusion that others are living ideal, perfect existences. When we examine our own behind-the-scenes struggles with others' highlight reels, we feel jealous, dissatisfied, or envious. This cycle reinforces the idea that we are "falling behind," which can lead to terrible emotional consequences.

The Envy Feedback Loop The relationship between self-criticism and jealousy bureaucracy is a self-perpetuating feedback loop. The more we evaluate ourselves against others, the more likely we are to feel green with envy or resentment. This, in turn, causes us to compare ourselves more, reinforcing our feelings of envy. The more we evaluate, the more we support the idea that we are not good enough or that others are superior.

**The role of cognitive biases:** Cognitive biases, including confirmation bias (the tendency to seek out evidence that confirms our beliefs), play a role in perpetuating the feedback loop of envy. When we feel envious, we routinely look for cues that reinforce the idea that others are more successful, attractive, or happy than we are. This selective interest increases our insecurities and reinforces the emotional cost of envy.

2. Freeing ourselves from the need to compete with others although social evaluation is a natural part of human behavior, it shouldn't dominate our lives or give rise to negative emotions like jealousy.

By recognizing the impact of evaluation and actively working to curb the need to compete, we will foster a better, more fulfilling relationship with others and ourselves.

1. Practice self-awareness and mindfulness. The first step to breaking free from comparison is to be open about how we communicate and engage in it. Mindfulness — the practice of listening to our mind and feelings without judgment — can help us discover moments when we are comparing ourselves to others. By noticing our feelings of envy or inadequacy, we will recognize the triggers and begin to break the cycle before it gets out of hand.
**Mindfulness Awareness:** Instead of suppressing or ignoring envy when we experience it, we will acknowledge it and look at its underlying causes. Mindfulness Ask yourself questions like,
"Why do I experience it this way?
What am I evaluating?
Is it wise to rate myself towards this person?"
Focusing allows us to step back and consider our feelings objectively, helping us to avoid getting caught in a cycle of poor self-talk and vice versa.
**Letting go of judgment:** Mindfulness also encourages us to allow ourselves to make judgments. Instead of labeling ourselves "bad" or "inferior" because of envy, we will present ourselves with compassion and knowledge. This shift in attitude can help reduce the emotional intensity of jealousy and allow us to respond to the feeling in a more positive way.
2. Shift from Comparison to Self-Reflection Instead of judging yourself against others, an additional empowering way is to focus on your own mirror image and private boom. Instead of asking,

"Why are they so much taller than me?"

ask yourself, "What can I learn from this person? How can I grow from this situation?"

**Celebrate your growth:** Shift your awareness from others to yourself. Celebrate your personal achievements, no matter how small, and replicate how far you've come. Everyone's journey is unique, and success seems unique to each man or woman. By seeing and appreciating your own progress, you reduce the urge to compare yourself to others.

**Set personal goals:** Instead of measuring your true worth to others, set your personal goals based solely on your values, passions, and desires. Personal goals help you stay focused on what matters most to you, whether it's building capacity, meeting career milestones, or improving your health and well-being. When you recognize your own accomplishments, comparisons clearly take a back seat.

3. Embrace abundance, not scarcity. Enough success, love, and joy to go around. When we realize that the successes of others no longer diminish our own potential, we free ourselves from the need to compete. Embracing abundance means that the success of others is not a threat to our own success.

**Support and celebrate others:** Instead of feeling jealous when someone else succeeds, try adopting a birthday-celebrating attitude. Supporting others and sharing in their joy can foster a sense of connection and connection rather than competition. When we sincerely wish others success, it lifts us up as well.

**Cultivate gratitude**: Focusing on what you have can shift your perspective from scarcity to abundance, as opposed to what you lack. Gratitude enables you to appreciate your specific strengths, accomplishments, and relationships, reducing the urge to judge and compete.

4. Limit social comparison triggers. In today's digital age, social evaluation is often driven by social media advertising. If you find that social media structures are constantly fueled by jealousy and envy, don't forget to set boundaries for the way you interact with them.

**Digital detox:** Taking regular breaks from social media can help you detach from the constant stream of comparisons and the curated, idealized images of others' lives. Use this time to create awareness for your own personal growth and well-being. Follow inspiring, enviable, accounts:

Refine your social media feeds by using the following accounts that inspire you and definitely contribute to your existence, replacing those that make you feel inferior.

Choose to interact with content that encourages you to follow your passions and enhance your lifestyle rather than fueling feelings of inferiority.

The work of evaluation in envy is deep, and it's easy to get caught up in the temptation to constantly measure yourself against others. However, by mastering the psychology behind social evaluation and the envy it creates, we can begin to break the cycle of opposition.

Self-focus, private reflection, abundance, and healthy digital behaviors can help us regain our consciousness, reduce envy, and foster an additional sense of happiness in our lives.

**1. The Danger of Envy in Professional Life**: How envy kills careers. Jealousy in the management center and its impact on professional fulfillment managing jealousy among colleagues and superiors the workplace is an environment where success, competition, and ambition intersect. While it can be an area for growth, innovation, and achievement, it is also a breeding ground for jealousy. The more a person strives for fulfillment, fame, and career advancement, the more likely they are to enjoy or witness feelings of jealousy. Envy in a professional environment, whether among colleagues or between subordinates and superiors, can be significantly negative. Not only for individuals, but also for teams, groups, and entire careers. Here, we will explore the dangers of jealousy within the workplace and the correct ways in which it harms career development, damages relationships, and creates a toxic environment. We can even discuss how to manage and reduce jealousy in professional settings, fostering healthier, more collaborative relationships that promote growth and success for all and sundry involved.

**1. Jealousy in the Workplace and Its Impact on Professional Success**

The workplace is regularly defined by opposition—opposition to promotions, raises, interest, and praise. While healthy competition can be stimulating, jealousy can quickly turn it toxic. When jealousy is allowed to fester in the workplace, it can have long-term consequences for both individuals and the company as a whole.

**The Cost of Jealousy on Career Development**

In competitive work environments, jealousy regularly emerges when a person perceives a threat to their personal prospects. This can result in feelings of inadequacy and resentment, ultimately hindering career advancement. Jealousy in the workplace can take many forms. Hostility, gossip, sabotage, or perhaps passive competitive behavior.

**Reduced focus and productivity:**

When employees are fed by jealousy, their interest and energy are diverted far from their own work.

Instead of focusing on their own desires and contributing to the success of the group, jealous employees may become preoccupied with the tasks of their colleagues. This distraction results in decreased productivity, poor choices, and lack of progress in their professional improvement.

**Missed opportunities for growth: Jealous** employees regularly resist collaboration and constructive feedback. Instead of seeing the success of others as an opportunity to learn and grow, they see it as a threat or as something, that highlights their own perceived shortcomings.

As a result, they may avoid seeking mentorship or guidance, forgo opportunities to explore new skills, and fail to develop necessary competencies.

**Self-sabotage and career stagnation:**
Jealousy can lead to self-sabotage, both through overt actions or by cultivating a mindset that prevents the jealous individual from engaging in their own first endeavors.

For example, they may intentionally undermine their personal paintings or fail to take difficult steps for fear of being overtaken by a more successful colleague. This stagnation hinders career development and prevents long-term growth.

Jealousy takes a huge emotional toll on mental health in the place of emotional tolcomam. It often stems from a lack of confidence, low self-esteem, or a fear of no longer measuring up.

Over time, these feelings can manifest as anxiety, stress, and burnout. Constantly evaluating yourself in front of others can erode self-esteem, which can lead to depression and chronic dissatisfaction.

**Stress and Anxiety: Jealousy** is a distressing emotion. It triggers the brain's fight-or-flight response, producing chemicals like cortisol that create stress and anxiety.

Over time, this stress can negatively impact a man or woman's mental and physical well-being, leading to burnout, sleep disruption, and negative choices.

**Poor focus and negative outlook:**

When an employee is consumed by jealousy, their mental energy is sapped by negative thoughts, reducing their ability to focus on the task. This clouded judgment often results in a pessimistic view of one's own potential, which in turn increases feelings of inadequacy.

Over time, this can lead to a cycle of negative self-talk that undermines the individual's well-being and professional development.

3. **The Impact of Jealousy on Workplace**

Relationships Workplaces are built on relationships—whether among colleagues, with superiors, or with subordinates. Jealousy can quickly sour these relationships, creating a toxic environment in which collaboration, consideration, and appreciation are eroded. When jealousy occurs, it can cause irreparable damage to professional networks, teamwork prospects, and the general way of life in the workplace. Jealousy among colleagues Among friends, jealousy regularly manifests itself as hostility, opposition, and backhanded compliments. It can damage the experience of friendship and teamwork, which is important for fulfillment in many businesses.

**Stress and hostility:**

Jealous employees may also engage in various (or no longer so subtle) acts of sabotage, including withholding facts, spreading rumors, or belittling the achievements of others. This behavior creates an environment of distrust, where people experience as if they cannot rely on their coworkers, in addition to damaging relationships. This anxiety makes it difficult to properly paint as a team, which reduces universal productivity and morale.

**Harming collaboration:**
Collaboration is a key factor in problem-solving, creativity, and productivity. However, jealousy prevents individuals from working together effectively. Jealous colleagues may not be willing to share skill sets, provide support, or celebrate the success of others, creating a divided environment that stifles innovation and growth.

**Gossip and Backbiting:** In the workplace, jealous people often resort to gossip to vent their frustrations or belittle the achievements of others. Now spreading malicious rumors not only hurts the target of the gossip but also damages the morale and morale of the entire team. Gossip triggers negative feelings, perpetuates the cycle of jealousy, and demotivates staff. Jealousy between subordinates and superiors Jealousy is not limited to interpersonal interactions. Friendly subordinates can also feel jealous of their supervisors, especially when a manager receives praise or recognition that they believe they deserve. Similarly, jealousy can arise when employees can rely on them to unfairly pass on promotions or recognition in favor of others.

**Stressed manager-employee relationships:**
Jealous employees may feel resentment toward their managers, especially if they perceive the supervisor as a favored plaything or an unfair reward. This resentment can result in passive-aggressive behavior, disengagement, and a lack of initiative in their roles. The manager, in turn, may even fight to motivate these employees or foster a strained working

relationship, which hinders group harmony and productivity.

**Perceived Inequality:**

Jealousy often arises when employees perceive that there is an inequality in the distribution of rewards, promotions, or benefits. If an employee feels that another is being favored for a promotion or opportunity, they will develop resentment toward the favored employee and their manager. This can lead to frustration, disengagement, and, in some cases, a desire to "get down" to those they perceive as incompetent.

**Lack of Respect and Authority:**

When jealousy exists between a supervisor and a subordinate, it can undermine the supervisor's authority. Employees who are jealous of their manager's position may openly criticize or disrespect their management, creating friction that affects overall staff performance and morale.

3. Managing Jealousy among Peers and Superiors

While jealousy is a natural human emotion; it must be carefully controlled in the workplace to avoid its adverse consequences. Employers, managers, and employees alike can take proactive steps to reduce jealousy and foster a more positive and supportive work environment.

1. Encourage open communication and transparency.

One important way to reduce jealousy in the workplace is through open communication. Encouraging employees to express their problems, frustrations, and desires can help you avoid misunderstandings and defuse competency conflicts.

**Regular feedback:** Employees who receive general, constructive remarks from their supervisors are much less likely to feel ignored or undervalued. Providing clear expectations, critiques of overall performance, and open discussions about professional improvement can help prevent jealousy from arising, as employees will feel extra secure in their positions.

**Recognizing Achievements:**
Celebrating employee accomplishments—both big in addition, small—creates an atmosphere of appreciation and recognition. When accomplishments are openly acknowledged, employees are less likely to feel jealous of others; because they can be assured that, their own efforts can be identified and rewarded.

2. Promoting cooperation over competition can encourage cooperation over competition. Help reduce conflicts and jealousy among colleagues. A team-oriented subculture, in which employees are validated for working together toward extraordinary goals, helps reduce the "me vs. them" mentality that often breeds jealousy.

**Team-building activities:**
Regular team-building activities, both formal and informal, can help foster a sense of unity and empathy. When employees work together on tasks or participate in team events, they foster mutual appreciation and knowledge, which reduces the likelihood of jealousy and coMentorship and Support: Providing mentorship opportunities allows employees to receive guidance and direction from more experienced peers. Encouraging senior employees to share their stories and accomplishments can help junior personnel see that success is an adventure, not a competition. Envy within the executive center can be devastating for both individuals and organizations. Whether it's damaging personal careers, fostering a toxic environment, or hindering collaboration, the

devastating effects of envy are far-reaching. However, by fostering open verbal exchanges, selling collaboration, and moving forward with compassion, workplaces can manage and reduce envy, creating environments that are supportive, effective, and conducive to fulfillment. By proactively addressing envy, employees and agencies can rework competition for healthy growth and development, ensuring that everyone has the opportunity to thrive.

## Chapter 13. The Spiritual Cure for Jealousy:

Finding Inner Peace and Contentment Spiritual Practices to Combat Jealousy Meditation, Gratitude, and Self-Reflection Envy, while a deeply human emotion, has the power to destroy not only our relationships and careers but also our inner peace. When we allow jealousy to fester, it creates an experience of imbalance and dissatisfaction within us, which blocks our path to authentic happiness and contentment. As we have discovered in previous chapters, the roots of jealousy are regularly found in insecurity, comparison, and unfulfilled desires. However, spiritual practices provide deeper tools for managing and, in the end, transcending these feelings. Spirituality, in its many guises, encourages us to connect with something greater than ourselves—whether it is better electricity, the universe, or our Higher Self. By working toward mindfulness, meditation, gratitude, and self-reflection, we will rework jealousy from a source of pain into an opportunity for growth and spiritual enrichment. In this chapter, we are able to explore various non-secular remedies for jealousy to help us cultivate inner peace, self-esteem, and contentment, drawing from non-secular traditions and teachings.

**1. Understanding the Spiritual Roots of Jealousy**

From a non-secular perspective, jealousy is often seen as a manifestation of deep feelings of lack—whether it be a lack of self-esteem, abundance, or connection to the divine. Many spiritual traditions teach that those feelings arise from the ego's desire to rule, compare, and compete, which causes us to forget our inner self and connection to the universe.

**Ego and Attachment:** In many Eastern traditions, including Buddhism and Hinduism, the ego is seen as the foundation of suffering. The ego thrives on attachment, evaluation, and opposition. Jealousy becomes an inevitable byproduct when we link our sense of true worth to outside examples or possessions. We ignore that real success comes from within and that we are all connected, no longer separate beings in competition with each other.

**Lack of faith:**

In religious spiritual traditions, jealousy can be seen as an indicator of spiritual imbalance, where we fail to believe in the divine plan for our lives. Instead of being content with what we have and trusting that everything will unfold as it should, we become fixated on what others have, believing that there is not enough to go around.

**Desire and Attachment:**
According to non-secular teachings like the Buddha, jealousy often stems from a desire to possess or control others. This yearning creates attachment, which, in turn, causes suffering. When we detach from these goals and attachments, we begin to create peace and attraction.

2. Spiritual Practices for Dealing with Jealousy
Dealing with Jealousy. By mastering the art of cultivating inner peace, letting go of ego-driven goals, and embracing compassion, we can free ourselves from the destructive grip of jealousy.

**1. Meditation:** Promoting Mindfulness and AcceptanceMeditation is one of the easiest non-secular ways to overcome jealousy. It helps to calm thoughts, develop self-awareness, and foster a sense of presence within the other. Through meditation, we can confront the root causes of our jealousy, allowing us to observe these feelings without judgment and, in the end, let them go. Mindfulness

**Meditation:** Mindfulness meditation, especially when practiced frequently, allows us to observe our mind and feelings as they arise. When jealousy appears, we tend to react. By quickly or suppressing the emotion, we can look at it with non-judgmental awareness. This helps us recognize the triggers of jealousy and create a space between the emotion and our reaction.

**Practice of Non-Attachment:**
Mindfulness additionally teaches non-attachment, helping us to understand that feelings of jealousy are timeless and do not define us. By working toward

non-attachment, we will look at our desires without being caught up in them, allowing us to let go of the urge to compare ourselves to others.

**Breathing Exercises:** In moments of envy, using deep, mindful breathing can help calm the fearful gadget and restore balance. By focusing on the breath, we take our attention away from the object of envy and back to the present moment, where peace resides.

**2. Gratitude:** Focusing from Lack to Abundance
Gratitude is a non-secular exercise that has the power to transform envy into contentment. When we focus on what we lack, we begin to shift our attitude from lack to abundance. Gratitude facilitates the experience of appreciating the benefits in our lives, making it easier to have a good time with the successes of others instead of being jealous.

**Gratitude Journaling:** Keeping a gratitude journal is a simple but effective way to combat envy. Every day, write down 3 things you are grateful for. These can be small or large things — your fitness, relationships, the beauty of nature, or the possibilities you have. Over time, this practice helps you to be more in tune with your life, making it less likely for envy to take root.

**Gratitude Meditation**: Another way to incorporate gratitude is through meditation. Start by sitting quietly and bringing to mind something or someone for whom you are very grateful. As you recognize this feeling of gratitude, allow it to expand throughout your frame and thoughts, filling you with warmth and appreciation. This practice helps you shift your energy from envy to joy.

**Seeing Others as a Mirror:** One effective way to use gratitude in the context of envy is to see others' accomplishments as a reflection of what is possible for you. Instead of feeling jealous of someone's achievements, recognize that their accomplishments are proof that similar possibilities and blessings are available to you. This attitude fosters a sense of community and shared abundance, reducing feelings of competition.

4. **Self-Reflection and Self-Inquiry:** Developing Inner Peace Self-reflection and self-inquiry are important tools in the spiritual journey of overcoming envy. By examining our feelings of envy, we are able to discover the deeper insecurities, fears, and goals that fuel these feelings. Self-reflection helps us develop greater self-awareness and compassion, allowing us to release the need for self-evaluation.

5. **Self-Inquiry Within the Advaita Vedanta Tradition:** In the philosophy of Advaita Vedanta, self-inquiry (called "atma vichara") is the practice of asking "Who am I?" and examining the character of the self. By delving deeper into the question of identity, we can understand that our authentic nature is beyond evaluation, beyond ego and past jealousy. The more we connect with our authentic selves, the less we will feel the need to judge ourselves by others.

6. **Journalism for Insight:** A powerful tool for self-reflection is journaling. Take the time to write down your feelings of jealousy and explore the underlying thoughts and beliefs that may be causing them.
Do you feel inadequate in some ways?
Do you believe that fulfillment is limited or that the successes of others diminish your own potential?
By considering these questions, you can begin to dissolve the ideas that perpetuate jealousy.
**Self-Confidence Affirmations:** Daily affirmations are another spiritual tool that can help combat

jealousy. Affirm your inner worth and right direction in life. Phrases like
"I am enough,"
"I trust the timing of my lifestyle,"
and "I have a good time"—the fulfillment of others as it inspires me—help reprogram your mind, shifting it away from envy and toward fame and gratitude.

### 3. The Power of Compassion and Loving-Kindness

**In** many spiritual traditions, cultivating compassion is seen as a way to dissolve negative emotions like jealousy. Compassion allows us to understand the interconnectedness of all beings and allows us to shift our perception from the ego to the heart. When we practice compassion, we are able to experience joy at the successes of others instead of envy. Loving-Kindness Meditation (Metta) Loving-Kindness meditation, or Metta Bhavana, is a Buddhist practice that involves sending feelings of goodwill, love, and compassion toward others. This practice allows the coronary heart to melt and dissolve the barriers of jealousy, promoting a sense of unity and interconnectedness.

**Sending love to others:**

In Metta meditation, you begin by directing loving-kindness toward yourself, then toward loved ones, friends, and then toward people you may be troubled by. The practice facilitates cultivating a mindset of goodwill and reduces the experience of competition or conflict.

**The practice of compassion:**

Compassion is not just a mental exercise. It is also about embodying kindness in action. When you act compassionately with others—offering help, listening attentively, or celebrating their victories—

you strengthen a sense of shared humanity, which reduces feelings of jealousy.

### 4. Letting Go of Attachment:

The Art of Detachment Many religious traditions emphasize the importance of detachment in overcoming negative emotions. Detachment does not mean detachment or forgetfulness. Instead, it refers to the ability to fully experience life without becoming overly attached to particular outcomes or possessions. By letting go of attachments, we free ourselves from the grip of jealousy. The Wisdom of Non-Attachment in Hinduism and Buddhism In both Hinduism and Buddhism, detachment is considered an important non-secular practice. In the Bhagavad Gita, Lord Krishna teaches Arjuna to behave without attachment to the results of his actions, emphasizing that true peace comes from focusing on the process rather than the outcome. Practicing non-attachment: In sensible terms, this means studying to become aware of one's own adventure without constantly judging others. Celebrate your own successes, but don't get too caught up in them. Similarly, examine the successes of others without attaching any judgment to them. Let go of the notion that others' successes are less than your own. Envy is a powerful emotion that, if left unchecked, can hinder our personal growth and secular improvement. However, through spiritual practices involving meditation, gratitude, self-reflection, compassion, and detachment, we can rework envy into an opportunity for inner growth and peace. By connecting with our true selves, practicing non-attachment, and cultivating a sense of abundance, we can distance ourselves from the negative consequences of envy and cultivate lasting contentment and joy. As we adopt these non-secular behaviors, we learn to live in harmony with ourselves and the sphere around us. By letting go of conflict and competition, we create the field for additional peace, love, and success in our non-public lives and in our interactions with others.

## Chapter 14: Healing from Envy:

Steps to Emotional Freedom Practical Strategies for Overcoming Envy The Importance of Forgiveness and Self-Compassion Envy is one of the most emotionally charged and unfavorable emotions we can experience. It can disrupt our private relationships, hinder our professional growth, and undermine our sense of self-esteem. When left untreated, envy can have a profound impact on both our emotional and physical well-being. Yet, the ability to heal from jealousy and free ourselves from its grip is not only doable but also essential to living a full and nonviolent lifestyle. Healing from jealousy requires a holistic approach of self-awareness, practical techniques, and a dedication to emotional freedom. This involves taking a step back to assess where jealousy comes from, acknowledging its effects, and then engaging in healing practices that promote emotional openness, forgiveness, and self-compassion.

This chapter will explore key steps for overcoming jealousy and creating a space for inner peace and emotional freedom.

1. Understanding Jealousy as an Opportunity for Healing Before embarking on a journey of recovery, it is crucial to recognize that jealousy, while painful, can be a powerful signal. It is often a reflection of deep emotional needs or unresolved concerns. Rather than seeing jealousy as a purely negative force, we are able to reframe it as a possibility for growth and change.

By addressing the underlying causes of jealousy, we can heal the wounds of the past and move forward with more emotional resilience.

**The Message Behind Jealousy**

Jealousy is often created through comparison—whether it's with a painting partner, a dating partner, or even a friend who seems to have what we need. It can stem from feelings of insecurity, unfulfilled desires, or inadequacy. In this sense, jealousy acts as a mirror, showing us where we experience bias or where we are overestimating external achievements.

**Insecurity and low self-esteem:**

Jealousy is often caused by a loss of self-esteem or a distorted experience of self-worth. When we feel like we're not enough or that others are "better" than us, we are vulnerable to feelings of jealousy. Recognizing that jealousy is a symptom of these deep insecurities can be the first step toward healing.

**Unmet Needs or Wants:**
Jealousy can also be an indication that our emotional or physical desires are not being met. Whether it's a desire for fame, love, success, or validation, jealousy often reflects an unmet need. Recognizing this need and finding healthy ways to fulfill it can shift the focus away from jealousy and toward self-empowerment. By seeing jealousy as an opportunity for emotional growth, we open the door to recovery and begin to develop important tools for emotional freedom.

2. Practical Strategies for Overcoming Jealousy
Overcoming jealousy requires both a change in mindset and practical techniques. The following sensible steps can help individuals eliminate unspoken jealousy and foster emotional freedom.

1. Develop self-awareness. The first step in recovering from jealousy is to focus on yourself. This method of becoming in tune with your emotional triggers involves paying attention to when jealousy arises, and exploring its root causes. Trace the triggers of jealousy: Start by journaling or reflecting on why and why jealousy arises. Are there any specific situations, people, or events that trigger feelings of jealousy? Is it the accomplishment of a chosen one, being perceived as mediocre, or the fear of missing something important? By learning what triggers your jealousy, you gain insight into the underlying cause of the emotion.
**Examine your beliefs:**

Often, jealousy is rooted in beliefs or distorted perceptions. For example, you may agree that there is a limited amount of success or happiness in the international, and if another person succeeds, it reduces your personal possibilities. By identifying these beliefs, you can begin to challenge and update them with healthier, more empowering thoughts. Observe without judgment: Instead of criticizing yourself for feeling jealous, practice looking at the emotion with interest and compassion. Recognize that feelings of jealousy are a natural part of being human, and they do not define you. By accepting and acknowledging your jealousy without judgment, you create space for healing.

2. Shift from comparison to appreciation. One of the most common sources of envy is evaluation. We often measure our success, glory, or worth against others, and envy arises when we perceive ourselves as lacking. To break free from this cycle of comparison, it is important to break free from this cycle of comparison.

**Celebrate the successes of others:**
Instead of viewing the successes of others as a threat, reframe them as a way of thinking. Celebrate the successes of others and let them inspire you instead of making your own experience inadequate. Recognizing that there can be enough success, love, and possibility for everyone can help dissolve feelings of opposition and competition.

**Focus on your own journey:**
Instead of comparing yourself to others, focus on your own direction. Reflect on your personal growth and the progress you have made, however small. By directing your energy

inward, you increase your sense of satisfaction and joy in your own, specific adventure.

**Practice gratitude:**

Gratitude is an effective antidote to jealousy. When you become aware of what you are grateful for in your personal existence, it becomes easier to allow jealousy to move. Keeping a gratitude journal or fulfilling gratitude practices day after day allows you to shift your attitude from lack to abundance.

2. Embrace vulnerability and self-compassion Healing from jealousy is also about healing. The underlying insecurities and wounds that fuel it. Practicing self-compassion and accepting vulnerability frees you from the self-loathing and guilt that often accompany jealousy.

**Self-compassion behaviors:**

Self-compassion involves treating yourself with the same kindness and understanding that you would provide to a loved one. When feelings of jealousy arise, respond with gentle skill, as opposed to criticizing yourself or feeling humiliated. Remind yourself that it's okay to feel jealous and that you are worthy of love and acceptance regardless of your feelings.

**Reframe vulnerability as strength:**

Vulnerability is often seen as a weak spot. However, in reality, it's an effective tool for emotional recovery. Allowing you to feel vulnerable in the face of jealousy—acknowledging your insecurities and fears—can be transformative. When you accept your vulnerability, you begin to let go of your need for outside validation and grow a deeper sense of self-worth.

1. Practice forgiveness. Forgiveness plays a vital role in healing from jealousy. Holding onto resentment or grudges, especially around those you feel jealous of, is very effective at fueling vulnerable feelings and perpetuating emotional struggles. Forgiveness doesn't mean condoning the behavior that fueled your jealousy. However, as an alternative, releasing the hold these feelings have on you can help you to let go of the feelings that you hold onto. Forgiving Yourself: Sometimes, the hardest character to forgive is ourselves. If you feel jealous because you agree that, you are no longer living up to your potential or that you are not being evaluated by others, practice forgiving yourself. Recognize that you are doing the best you can with the knowledge and assets you have at the moment. Allow yourself to heal and move forward.

**Forgiving Others:**

When jealousy is directed at others—whether it is a partner, a colleague, or a friend—it is important to let go of any bitterness or resentment. Addressing negative emotions directly is what keeps you attached to jealousy. Forgiving others frees you from emotional baggage and creates space for healing.

**Forgiveness Meditation:**

Practicing forgiveness meditation can be an effective way to release jealousy. Start by visualizing the person or person you are jealous of, then mentally offer them forgiveness. You will likely say, "I forgive you, and I release the hold you have on my heart." Then, turn that forgiveness inward, providing it to yourself. This practice can significantly reduce feelings of jealousy and promote emotional freedom.

5. Let go of expectations and control.

Jealousy often arises when we feel that something is "unfair" or that life is not going according to plan. The preference to manipulate outcomes or expectations can make us feel powerless, which leads to frustration and jealousy. By learning to let go of rigid expectations, we will let go of the desire to compare and manage.

**Embrace imperfection:**

Life is messy and unpredictable, and things do not always go according to our expectations. By embracing lifestyle imperfections, we can allow stress to be fought, controlled, or measured. Recognize that everyone has the right direction and that everything unfolds in its own time.

**Trust the process:**

Trusting that things are unfolding, as they should can help start the anxiety and jealousy that comes from feeling left behind. Believe that there will come a time and that there can be enough room in the world for everyone to be and succeed.

2. The Importance of Emotional Freedom in Long-Term Healing from Jealousy Emotional Freedom.

By releasing jealousy and its hold on your heart, you free yourself from the emotional burden that prevents you from fully embracing life again. Emotional freedom allows you to experience true peace, joy, and success, unencumbered by the need for evaluation or external validation.

**Living Authentically:**

When we let go of jealousy, we open ourselves up to living authentically. Without the constant desire to measure ourselves against others, we can pursue our dreams, goals, and passions with an experience of self-assurance. We can live in alignment with our proper values, unencumbered by the barriers of contradiction.

**Deepening Relationships**:

When we are free from jealousy, our relationships with others deepen. We can celebrate the success of others without feeling threatened, fostering an atmosphere of agreement, support, and mutual respect. By focusing on the collective good, we strengthen our relationships with others and contribute to a more harmonious world. Healing from jealousy is a path to emotional freedom. It requires self-awareness, forgiveness, compassion, and a change in attitude. By seeing jealousy as a potential for growth and addressing the underlying insecurities and unmet needs that fuel it, we are able to free ourselves from its grip. Through mindful strategies that include gratitude, self-compassion, and letting go of expectations, we can heal emotionally and create space for inner peace, happiness, and success. When we let go of jealousy, we open ourselves up to a life of authenticity, connection, and emotional freedom.

# Chapter 15: Creating Awareness:

Teaching children how to deal with jealousy.

Developing strategies for dealing with jealousy in children creating a healthy emotional environment at home Envy is a natural and often uncomfortable emotion, but it is an emotion that all children (and adults) will experience at some point. For young people, jealousy often arises in situations where they believe someone else has something they want—whether it is attention, toys, a prize, or a skill they would like to possess. Left unchecked, jealousy can lead to resentment, opposition, or even emotional difficulties.

As parents or caregivers, one of the most important things we can do is teach young people how to understand, manage, and express their jealousy in healthy ways. Doing so not only helps them navigate this particular emotion, but also equips them with important emotional regulation skills that will enable them to process other difficult emotions throughout their lives. Here is a comprehensive guide to raising awareness about jealousy and teaching children how to handle it in a positive and compassionate way.

1. **Recognize and normalize feelings of jealousy**

   The first step in helping young people deal with jealousy is to recognize that it is a regular, natural emotion. Instead of ignoring or minimizing their feelings, parents should take some time to validate them. Validate the emotion: It is important for children to recognize that jealousy is not "scary" or something to feel ashamed of. Instead, it is a normal emotion that everyone experiences.

   Reassure your child by saying something like, "I understand that you are feeling jealous right now, and that's okay. Everyone feels jealous from time to time, even adults."

   **Normalizing jealousy:** When children enjoy jealousy, they may feel that they are the ones who are most vulnerable to feeling this way or that their feelings are wrong. By explaining that jealousy is a normal human emotion, you reduce the chances of them feeling isolated or misunderstood. Share examples of the way you have felt jealousy on the outside and the way you handled it.

   **Encourage emotional awareness:** Teach your young child the language to describe their feelings. Help them identify a range of colors in their emotional experience rather than simply labeling their feelings as "scary" or "true."

For example, "It seems like you are feeling jealous because your sister is getting more attention right now. Can you tell me what that feels like on your body? What is going on inside?"

2. **Model healthy emotional responses Children**

   Explore how adults around them handle their emotions. If parents or caregivers are able to devise healthy ways to manage jealousy, the young person is more likely to adopt these strategies themselves to cope.

   **Show emotional regulation:**
   When you feel jealous or angry, instead of hiding or suppressing it, talk about it openly in a calm and controlled way. For example, if you feel jealous of a partner's success, you might say to your child, "I'm feeling a little burned out right now, but I'm going to take a deep breath and be mindful of what I want." This helps young people recognize that feelings of jealousy don't have to lead to a bad or harmful reaction.

   **Reinforce self-soothing techniques:**
   Demonstrating how to calm you when faced with jealousy is an important lesson for children. This can include taking a few deep breaths, walking away from the jealousy-inducing situation, or having a genuine conversation with someone you agree with. Encourage your child to implement these strategies, too,

whenever they experience a crush that is fueled by jealousy.

**Discuss emotional resilience:** Share examples of ways you've worked through difficult emotions like jealousy or envy. "I practically felt jealous when a friend of mine was advertised on paintings. But instead of letting that discourage me, I targeted the issues that might be going well in my lifestyle and used it as motivation to work harder in the direction of my personal dreams.

3. Teach empathy and perspective-taking. One of the best ways to help an infant overcome jealousy is to teach them how to remember the feelings and perspectives of others.

**Put yourself in someone else's shoes:** Encourage your toddler to consider the better state of the situation. If they are jealous of a friend's new toy, ask, "How do you feel about your friend getting this new toy? Do you observe that they worked hard to get it? How would you feel if someone envied you something you worked hard for?"

**Build empathy:** Use jealousy as an opportunity to teach empathy. This might involve asking your child how they might feel if their sibling received extra attention or praise. By considering how their jealousy might affect the other person, they will begin to understand that their feelings are not isolated to themselves, and that jealousy can cause harm or distress.

**Celebrating the success of others:** Teach your young child to be happy for others' accomplishments or genuine good fortune, rather than seeing it as an opportunity.

For example, if a classmate wins an award, encourage them to express specific praise rather than dwelling on their own feelings of loss or inadequacy. "Isn't it first class that your friend got an award? What makes you think he's so right about it?"

4. **Encourage open communication about feelings.**

    Children often internalize emotions that they don't understand or feel are too difficult to express. Creating a safe, non-judgmental environment at home where feelings can be shared boldly is important for helping children with jealousy.

    **Encourage open communication:** If your child is feeling jealous, help them verbalize it. Instead of telling them to avoid feelings of jealousy, invite them to be in tune with their mind and emotions.

    "You seem unhappy. Do you want to talk about what's bothering you?" This suggests to your little one that they can express all manner of emotions and that talking about them is part of working through them. Listen without judgment: Sometimes, children just need to be heard. Instead of responding or dismissing their feelings, focus on being practical. Let them explain why they're feeling jealous and reassure them that it's okay to have strong feelings.

**Use stories and books:**
Books are a great way to help children understand emotions like jealousy. There are many children's books that are designed to educate and build emotional intelligence. Reading testimonies about characters who deal with jealousy can offer both insight and reassurance in your child.

5. **Help develop problem-solving skills.**
Once your child has learned to understand their jealousy and the emotional impact it has, the next step is to help them find positive ways to manage it.

**Focus on the solution:**
After acknowledging the feeling, guide your little one toward a solution. Ask questions like, "What can we do to feel better when this happens?" or "How can we handle this in a way that makes us proud of our accomplishments?" Encourage them to think about what they can do when jealousy arises, including taking advantage of something, focusing on their own accomplishments, or practicing patience.

**Encourage reflection:**

Help your child reflect on the reasons for their jealousy. Does it feel like they are being ignored? Are they upset because they are not getting enough attention? When children can identify the source of their jealousy, they may be better able to manage it.

**Provide constructive feedback:** If your toddler is acting out jealously, help them learn how they can deal with similar situations in the future. This can include role-playing or discussing specific events in which jealousy is likely to arise and working toward how they can respond more positively or thoughtfully.

6. **Create a balanced environment at home**

   A healthy emotional environment at home supports the development of emotional intelligence and self-regulation in children. By fostering great interactions and managing the emotional ecosystem, parents can help reduce feelings of jealousy and resentment.

   **Promote a positive family culture:** Establish an environment in which praise, kindness, and appreciation are prioritized. Hold regular family conferences to talk about feelings, celebrate each other's accomplishments, and encourage well-behaved teams.

   Limit comparisons: Children clearly compare themselves to others, especially siblings or peers. Make it a point to focus on their male or female strengths and achievements as opposed to judging others.

For example, instead of pronouncing, "Why can't you be extra like your brother?" Spotlight what makes your little one special. "You're undoubtedly innovative, and we love how you saw outside the container!"

**Encourage cooperation over competition:**

Create opportunities for children to work collectively rather than compete. Cooperative games, group-based work, and shared play help children feel connected and supportive rather than distant and aggressive.

This reduces jealousy and promotes teamwork and shared happiness.

7. **Promote self-compassion and healthy self-esteem.**

Teaching children to develop a positive self-concept is crucial to reducing jealousy. When young people feel secure. Own each member's specific contributions. This builds their sense of personal worth and self-esteem, making them less likely to be consumed by feelings of jealousy.

**Self-compassion techniques**:

Teach your child that it's okay to experience imperfections or have feelings of jealousy, but they should allow these feelings to shape their self-esteem. Use positive affirmations and encourage self-compassion. Say, "It's okay to be jealous sometimes; however, you are valuable and special just the way you are."

**Focus on growth, not perfection:**

Encourage a growth mindset that emphasizes effort and progress. Praise your child's perseverance and skill, prioritizing only the results they achieve. This helps young people become aware of their own adventures rather than constantly evaluating themselves in front of others. Teaching children how to manage jealousy involves acknowledging their feelings, developing emotional intelligence, and providing them with the tools to deal with these feelings and transform them into productive behaviors. By normalizing jealousy, modeling healthy responses, building empathy, and creating a positive and supportive emotional environment, parents can help children navigate this difficult emotion in a way that promotes emotional growth, resilience, and appropriate well-being. Helping young people deal with jealousy isn't just about stopping bad behaviors. It's about empowering them with the skills they need to effectively manage all of their emotions, ultimately leading to a more compassionate, self-aware, and emotionally intelligent generation.

## Chapter 16. The Role of Empathy in Managing Jealousy

Empathy and Knowledge Reduce Jealousy Promote Emotional Intelligence. Jealousy is a complex emotion that can cause massive strain in relationships, whether romantic, familial, or social. It often stems from a lack of trust, fear of loss, or hostility toward others. However, empathy—the ability to recognize and share the emotions of others—plays a critical role in coping with and managing these feelings. By developing a deeper sense of empathy, individuals can address the root causes of jealousy, cultivate emotional resilience, and build stronger, healthier relationships.

1. **How empathy and understanding help reduce jealousy.**

Empathy is a powerful tool that helps us move beyond the self-centered emotions of jealousy. By seeing the state of affairs from another character's perspective, we gain additional insight into both our own and others' emotions. This deeper understanding can reduce the depth of jealousy and allow for more empathetic, constructive responses.

**Perspective taking:**

One of the key ways empathy works to reduce jealousy is perspective taking. When we empathize with someone, we put ourselves in his or her shoes and try to see the situation through their eyes.

For example, if we feel jealous of a colleague's advancement, empathy allows us to understand that their accomplishment is the result of their hard work and achievements, not something that reduces our own paycheck. This shift from evaluation to mastery helps reduce feelings of competition or resentment.

**Understanding the Roots of Insecurity**:

Many jealous feelings are linked to underlying insecurity or fears of inadequacy. Empathy allows us to understand the inner struggles within ourselves and others.

Moreover, empathy enables us to recognize that our insecurities are not inherently terrible but are part of the human experience.

This knowledge can reduce the negative impact of jealousy and prevent it from controlling our actions.

**Empathy instead of jealousy:**

Empathy fosters empathy, shifting our focus from jealousy to understanding. Instead of seeing everyone else's success as a threat to our own, we begin to see it as a possibility for connection and guidance. For example, when we empathize with a chum Who is in a satisfying court, instead of being threatened, we are able to rejoice in their happiness and appreciate that their happiness does not take anything away from our own lifestyle or relationship.

**Conflict Resolution:**

In romantic or non-public relationships, jealousy regularly arises from miscommunication or unfulfilled emotional desires. Empathy plays a key role in resolving these conflicts by encouraging open and honest conversation. By listening to each other's fears and weaknesses, partners can learn where jealousy is coming from, paint together to solve problems, and improve our relationship. Empathy enables us to transform jealousy from a negative emotion into a possibility for mutual growth.

2. **How developing emotional intelligence can help you overcome jealousy.**

    Emotional intelligence (EI) - the ability to perceive, understand, and control both your own feelings and the feelings of others - is essential for reducing jealousy. Developing EI helps people approach jealousy with greater mindfulness, regulation, and empathy, leading to healthier relationships and personal growth. Developing emotional intelligence involves several components that can be developed through practice.

    **Self-awareness:**

    The first step in overcoming jealousy is recognizing that we are experiencing it. Emotional intelligence encourages self-focus, helping us to grasp our emotional triggers. When we experience jealousy, EI allows us to reflect on why we are feeling this way. Are we feeling insecure about our personal accomplishments? Are we afraid of letting down someone important to us? By identifying the root causes of jealousy, we will more effectively address these emotions as opposed to letting them control our actions.

    **Self-regulation:**

Emotional intelligence additionally involves controlling our emotions, as opposed to letting them take over. When jealousy arises, it can be tempting to react quickly—through accusations, withdrawal, or non-competitive behavior. However, emotional intelligence teaches us how to pause, defuse, and choose a measured response. This may include taking time to calm down, journaling about feelings of jealousy, or discussing the feelings with the involved character in a positive way. By doing so, we protect ourselves from negative relationships with jealousy and allow for more healthy communication.

**Empathy for Others:**
Empathy is the cornerstone of emotional intelligence. Being able to tune into the emotions and experiences of others not only deepens relationships but also helps to move past jealousy. When we understand that others have their own struggles, fears, and goals, we are less likely to view their success or happiness as a personal threat. Instead, we will appreciate their adventures and their percentage of happiness, which facilitates the dissolution of feelings of jealousy and promotes mutual support.

**Social skills:**
Cultivating emotional intelligence also increases the ability to navigate social interactions in a way that promotes agreement and cooperation.

For example, when we experience jealousy in a relationship, emotional intelligence helps us communicate our feelings in a way that is respectful and open. Instead of blaming others, we make our personal desires and feelings perfectly clear, which promotes speaking up and understanding. These social skills reduce the potential for jealousy to escalate into a fight.

**Positive thinking:**

Emotional intelligence involves creating situations where jealousy is likely to arise, from a beneficial perspective. Rather than viewing someone's success or closeness as a personal threat, the wearable frame views the situation as a potential for personal growth. If a partner is spending time with friends, we can see it as an opportunity to strengthen our friendships by venting our feelings. This shift in behavior helps us manage jealousy in a healthy way and allows us to sense the happiness of others without feeling deprived.

3. Practical strategies for developing empathy and emotional intelligence Developing empathy and emotional intelligence is a slow process that requires practice and mindfulness.

There are a number of practical techniques that will allow you to strengthen these skills, making it less complicated to manage feelings of jealousy and build more meaningful connections with others.

**Active listening:**
One of the best ways to actively engage in empathy at home. When we focus attentively, without interruption or judgment, we open ourselves to learning more deeply about others. In the context of jealousy, active listening allows us to hear and validate the feelings of others, which in turn can help reduce misunderstandings and build trust. Practice being present in a conversation and paying full attention to the feelings of the other character.

**Mindfulness and reflection:**
Mindfulness exercises, including meditation or deep breathing physical games, allow you to live a grounded life and become aware of your feelings. When jealousy arises, mindfulness enables you to study your emotions without using them to kill them. By reflecting on the source of your jealousy, you can clarify whether it is insecurity, worry, or something else.

**Journaling:**
Writing down your stories and feelings can be a helpful way to process feelings of jealousy. Journaling allows you to explore your mind in a safe, nonjudgmental space, which can help you uncover the root causes of your jealousy and allow you to grow emotionally. It can also serve as a tool for self-reflection, which can help you become aware of your own behavioral patterns and how you have responded to jealousy in the past.

**Engage in perspective taking:**
Make a conscious effort to put yourself in the other person's shoes. This can be as simple as imagining the situation from the person's perspective as you experience jealousy.

For example, if a colleague receives an award for their work, rather than feeling resentful, try to respect their effort and acknowledge the hard work they put in to earn that recognition. This practice not only allows for a reduction in jealousy but also increases feelings of gratitude and belonging.

**Empathetic communication:**
When discussing jealousy with a partner, friend, or colleague, it is important to use language that promotes understanding rather than defensiveness. Use "I" statements as opposed to "you" statements to avoid accusations.

For example, instead of declaring, "You always spend more time with your friends than necessary," say, "I feel neglected when we don't spend as much time together." This approach invites empathy and opens the door to hopeful conversations. Empathy is an important tool for overcoming jealousy because it allows us to see beyond our own fears and insecurities, helping us to understand the feelings and thoughts of others. By cultivating emotional intelligence — which includes self-awareness, self-regulation, and empathy — individuals respond to jealousy more appropriately, fostering stronger, more trusting relationships. Whether you are coping with jealousy in romantic dating, at work, or within a friendship, empathy can reframe this potentially negative emotion into an opportunity for non-public escalation and emotional connection.

## Chapter 17: Jealousy within the Digital Age:

The Rise of Social Media and Jealousy How Social Media Fuels Feelings of Jealousy Navigating the Virtual World Without Being Jealousy The modern, virtual global, social media has added an extraordinary amount of pressure to our lives. It has reshaped the way we connect, speak, and even understand ourselves and others. While social media brings possibilities for personal expression, connection, and entertainment, it has also given rise to new types of emotional distress, most notably jealousy and envy. With the constant flow of photos and updates, social media systems like Instagram, Facebook, TikTok, and Twitter can fuel feelings of insecurity, inadequacy, and competition. This is largely due to the curated and idealized variations of people's lives that we are constantly exposed to, which causes us to compare our reality to the glimpses of others.

Understanding how social media fuels jealousy and finding ways to mentally navigate this virtual world is crucial to maintaining emotional well-being.

1. How Social Media Fuels Feelings of Envy Social media systems are visually designed to encourage engaging and collaborative interaction. They thrive on the influx and sharing of content that often highlights the most glamorous, hits, or enviable moments of existence. This environment can create major feelings of envy, especially when users are constantly bombarded with highlights of others'

lives. Here's how social media specifically feeds these impoverished feelings:

**Highlight Reels vs. Real Life:** The Distorted Reality of Social Media One of the number-one drivers of envy on social media is users' tendency to post their "highlight reels"—carefully crafted, staged, and repeatedly edited moments that present an idealized snapshot of their lives. Whether it's a picture-perfect vacation, a new home, a wonderful opportunity, or a milestone achievement, those moments rarely replicate the struggles, complications, or ordinary moments that make up most human lives. This creates a distorted reality where it seems like everyone else is living a more exciting, glamorous, or successful existence. When we compare these idealized images to our own "behind the scenes" truth, it can lead to feelings of inadequacy, self-doubt, and jealousy. We may also begin to experience that our own lives are lacking or that we are not measuring up to the seemingly perfect lives of others.

**The Illusion of Perfection:**

Filters, Editing, and Unrealistic Expectations Social media structures, especially visual-based structures like Instagram and Snapchat, are built around images and films, which can be regularly edited, filtered, or staged to make them look more polished. People typically provide a model of themselves that is not entirely real, using filters to smooth out flaws, adjust lighting, and embellish physical abilities. While it is often done for artistic or aesthetic purposes, it can create unrealistic grandeur needs and lifestyle expectations. When we compare ourselves to these "perfect" images, it can trigger feelings of envy and protection, especially if we feel we don't meet these unrealistic demands. How to Really Get It.

**Fear of Missing Out (FOMO):**
The Pressure to Keep Up Another thing that fuels envy and social media is the phenomenon of FOMO – or "being anxious." Social media is constantly updated with new content, featuring friends, influencers, celebrities, and peers attending events, traveling, or living seemingly happy and social lifestyles. This can trigger feelings of exclusion, as if everyone is engaged in reviews that we are not. FOMO can be especially strong when we see others accomplish milestones—like getting a promotion, buying a brand new car, or going on a dream vacation—while we experience a sense of being "stuck" in our own state of being. This worry about not being noticed or measuring up to others' experiences can quickly turn into jealousy, especially if we experience that we lack something great.

**The Social Comparison Trap:**
Constant Exposure to Others' Success Human nature is wired for social inconsistency. We regularly compare our own personal well-being and achievements to the teeth, which is handstamped on social media. Whether it's looking at a friend's excellent relationships, a colleague's professional advancement, or an acquaintance's glamorous lifestyle, these comparisons regularly lead to negative feelings of envy. In fact, studies show that humans are more likely to evaluate themselves upward (i.e., to those they consider "better" or more successful) than downward (those they consider "lesser" or suffering). These upward comparisons often lead to envy, because people can also feel inadequate in their evaluation of others' achievements or lives. The more we look at others' achievements, the more we are willing to experience

that we are falling short in a number of ways.

**Validation and Approval:**
Pressure to gain external validation Social media has also become a validation tool through likes, shares, and feedback. Many people post content in the hope of receiving likes or great comments from others, and this can create a cycle of dependence on external approval. When a person receives a high number of likes or shares, it can validate their sense of self-worth, while those whose posts are ignored may feel ignored or inferior. This can fuel jealousy, especially when we examine how much attention we receive online for the apparent success of others' posts. In this digital lifestyle, self-esteem and validation are linked to social media interactions, heightened feelings of jealousy, and self-esteem.

2. Navigating the virtual world without being jealous While social media can regularly fuel feelings of jealousy, there are conscious ways to navigate the virtual world without letting jealousy get out of hand. It's about putting barriers in place, promoting healthy behaviors, and proactively working to uncover jealousy-inducing content. Here are strategies that can help:

**Practice digital detoxing:**
Disconnect for mental clarity One of the most effective ways to combat jealousy and envy is to take a daily break from social media. A digital detox—even if it's for a few hours, today, or tomorrow—helps you declutter your intellectual kingdom and reduce the constant pressure to keep up with the lives of others. During this time, you can focus on real-world stories and interactions, reducing the risk of diagnosis and emotional burnout. Digital detoxes now not only give your

brain a break but also allow you to reconnect with yourself and your own accomplishments, without the pure noise.

**Limit time on social media:**
Be intentional about mindless scrolling. Setting limits on how much time you spend on social media can help reduce the temptation to endlessly scroll through your feed with ads. You can use apps that can block your usage or specific times to view your accounts during the day. By using social media with a purpose, rather than aimlessly scrolling, you're much less likely to fall into the land of the opposite or self-complaining. Limiting time on social media also allows you to identify more offline activities that express happiness and success, including fun, relationships, and self-care practices.

**Mindfully curate your feed:**
Follow content that promotes growth. Another way to navigate social media mindfully is to help transform your feed into a mirror of content that is positive, inspiring, and aligned with your non-public values. Instead of following unrealistic beauty standards or lifestyle peddling, choose to follow pages that encourage self-improvement, mindfulness, and personal growth. Accounts that frame positivity, mental wellness, or creativity can provide a more suitable opportunity for the circulation of idealized images and quality content. If some bulls make you feel terrible about yourself or trigger jealousy, don't hesitate to unfollow or mute them — you'll have to manipulate the content you consume. Shift from comparison to inspiration: Using social media as a growth tool Instead of comparing yourself to others, try reframing what you see on social media as an opportunity for ideas rather than a source of jealousy.

For example, if you see someone accomplishing something you admire, use it as motivation to set your own personal dreams. Instead of feeling jealous of someone else's accomplishments, have a good time with their achievements and allow them to inspire you to do the same in your own personal life. This mindset shift allows you to use social media as a tool for self-growth and growth rather than a breeding ground for envy.

**Focus on gratitude:**
Shifting your mindset from scarcity to abundance Gratitude is one of the most effective antidotes to envy. When you practice gratitude, you shift your awareness to what you already have. If you find yourself resentful of someone else's accomplishments or lifestyle, take a moment to reflect on the high-quality aspects of your own being. Cultivating a gratitude practice—whether by keeping a daily journal or reflecting on what you're grateful for—will help you develop a more effective and balanced attitude. Gratitude helps you realize that there is plenty of success, love, and happiness to go around and that someone else's good fortune does not diminish you.

**The Impact of Social Media on Your Self-Esteem:**
Separating Virtual and Real-World Validation The most important lesson in navigating social media without becoming a victim of envy is to recognize that your self-esteem is not determined by external validation. Social media impressions, including likes, comments, or shares, can be fleeting and unreliable as indicators of your true worth. Instead of basing your vanity on online interactions, focus on building a sense of worth that comes from within through your relationships, achievements, personal growth, and values. When you separate your self-

esteem from social media validation, it becomes less difficult to engage with it without using envy to crush it.

**Engage in authentic interactions:**
Foster real-world connections. Finally, instead of passively staring at the curate lives of others, take the time to engage with social media in a genuine and meaningful way. Leave thoughtful comments, give your personal reviews, and connect with others who share similar interests or values.

This type of interaction fosters a sense of community and authenticity that can counteract the superficiality that often fuels jealousy.

By focusing on real connections rather than comparisons, you can cultivate a healthier social media presence. Social media has undoubtedly changed the way we interact with the sector, but it also brings with it new challenges, especially among those who are prone to jealousy and envy.

Curated content, constant comparisons, and pressure to meet unrealistic standards can all contribute to feelings of inadequacy and resentment.

However, by working on mindfulness, improving your online enjoyment, mastering gratitude, and separating your self-esteem from digital validation, you can navigate social media in a more appropriate, more balanced way. Instead of letting social media fuel jealousy, you can use it as a tool for imagination, connection, and personal growth, which ultimately leads to a more enjoyable and fulfilling existence.

# Chapter 18: The Power of Gratitude:

Transforming Jealousy into Appreciation Practicing gratitude can neutralize jealousy. Shifting Awareness from Lack to Abundance Jealousy is a natural, yet often harmful, emotion that stems from feelings of inadequacy, fear of loss, or envy of others' possessions, achievements, or relationships. It can create anxiety in relationships, hinder personal growth, and diminish feelings of happiness and self-worth. However, one effective device for re-modeling jealousy that is far more beneficial is gratitude.

Developing a gratitude practice may not neutralize feelings of envy at best. However, it additionally shifts our attitude from one of scarcity to one of abundance.

By appreciating what we have, we ultimately foster more contentment, compassion, and joy in the way we view others, and ourselves ultimately fostering more contentment, compassion, and joy in our lives.

**1. How Practicing Gratitude Can Neutralize Envy.** Gratitude is the practice of finding and appreciating the great things in our lives, no matter how small. This awareness of what is lacking in a gift, and this shift in focus, can significantly reduce the grip of envy. When we consciously practice gratitude, we are better able to recognize our personal strengths, achievements, and blessings, which is the lack of envy or the jealousy that often accompanies envy. **Reframing Perspective:** Envy is often triggered by the idea that someone else has something that we lack—whether it's fulfillment, glory, love, or material possessions. When we practice gratitude, we begin to reframe our thinking. Instead of focusing on what we don't have, gratitude facilitates our awareness of what we already have. By acknowledging abundance in our personal lives, we will allow the false notion that "there's not enough anymore" to move on. For example, if we feel jealous of a colleague's progress, working toward gratitude for our own personal career achievements, talents, or potential facilitates us to honor our own personal adventure and success. We begin to see that there can be ample room for everybody to flourish.

**Shifting from envy to inspiration:**
Gratitude encourages us to appreciate and fulfill the benefits of others rather than seeing them as an opportunity. When we practice gratitude, we will succeed in being motivated by the passion of another person.

For example, if a friend achieves something we desire—like running a marathon or shopping for a brand new car—rather than feeling jealous, we can choose to celebrate their success and allow ourselves to be motivated.

Gratitude allows us to recognize the value of others' reviews without being diminished by their help.

**Emotional Regulation:**
Envy often triggers strong emotional responses like resentment, disappointment, or frustration. By cultivating the practice of gratitude, we will increase our emotional regulation skills. Gratitude allows us to be more aware of our emotional state and gives us the tools to change the narrative in our minds. When we feel a surge of envy, taking a moment to reflect on the things we are grateful for can help us regain emotional stability and shift our energy from negative emotions to positive ones. This practice of mindful gratitude serves as an effective emotional restorer.

**Increased Self-Esteem:**
At the heart of envy is often a lack of self-confidence or a fear that we are not enough. Practicing gratitude for our own lives, achievements, and qualities helps, we build our sense of self-esteem. When we recognize the specific qualities and strengths we possess, we are less likely to compare ourselves to others. By focusing on the great things about our lives, and ourselves we reduce the desire to seek external validation or to judge ourselves in front of others.

3. **Focusing on Lack to Abundance**
A central element of gratitude is the shift from a mindset of scarcity — the idea that there is never enough of something around us — to a mindset of abundance, which recognizes that we can all have more. This shift is important for overcoming jealousy because it frees us from the scarcity mindset that often fuels feelings of competition and evaluation. Here's how cultivating an abundance mindset can turn jealousy into appreciation:

**Recognizing Abundance in Our Lives:**
When we are conscious of what we already have instead of what we don't, we begin to see the abundance around us. This can be anything from appreciating the love of our family and friends, recognizing our talents and abilities, or being grateful for excellent health. Gratitude helps us see the richness in our lives, even if it is no longer usually considered in external circumstances that we envy.

For example, instead of feeling jealous of someone's beautiful outing, we can appreciate the time we spend with the people we love, the stories we already have, or the opportunities we already have, people. This acknowledgement of abundance reduces the emotional charge of envy because we see that we are already adequately provided for in many ways.

**Challenging the scarcity mindset:**
Envy is often driven by the idea that a limited amount of fulfillment, love, or happiness can be most effective in going around.

For example, we may assume that if a partner shows affection to someone else, it means that less love is available to us. Similarly, if a spoonful achieves something we desire, we will feel that it is "too little" of an achievement for us. Gratitude challenges this scarcity mindset by showing us that there is always enough to go around. Success is not a finite resource, and the happiness or success of one character does not diminish our own capacity for fulfillment. By focusing on abundance in our personal lives and recognizing that there is room for everyone, we will reduce feelings of competition or envy.

**Appreciating the journey, not just the destination:** Gratitude helps us recognize the techniques for growth and self-improvement, no longer just the result. When we are caught up in envy, we often focus on the results that others have achieved (including the promotion, new car, or perfect date), but we forget the cost of our own journey.

By shifting our focus to gratitude, we can appreciate the steps we have taken, the lessons we have discovered, and the personal growth we have experienced. This shift is being able to recognize where we are now, rather than feeling resentful about where others are. It reminds us that our course is specific and that the reports we are going through are valuable in their own right.

**Gratitude for the Successes of Others:**
Instead of resenting the successes of others, gratitude can help us embrace the successes of those around us. When we practice gratitude, we recognize that someone else's successes do not take away from our own potential for fulfillment. There is enough room in the world for everyone to succeed, and their success can serve as a springboard for our personal growth. Practicing gratitude for the successes of others creates an experience of connection and celebration rather than jealousy and competition. For example, if a friend gets a promotion, we are able to feel genuinely happy for them, recognizing that their success does not diminish our own potential for fulfillment.

**Abundance in Relationships:**
In relationships, jealousy is often accompanied by fear of losing someone's love or attention to every other man or woman. Gratitude can help us to remember the flow and connection that exists in our lives. Whether it's the love of family, friends, or a partner, practicing gratitude helps us honor the relationships we already have, as opposed to fearing their loss. When we feel secure in the love and support we receive, we're less likely to feel threatened by others or to take ownership in our relationships.

4. **Practical Tips for Cultivating Gratitude to Replace** Jealousy Developing a gratitude practice isn't a one-day process; however, with consistency and purpose, it can transform the way we see the world and our place in it. Here are some practical guidelines that will help you turn gratitude and jealousy into appreciation.

**KeepaGratitudeJournal:**

Writing down the things, you are grateful for every day is an effective way to cultivate gratitude. This practice trains your mind to recognize the wonderful elements of your lifestyle and shifts your attitude from what is overwhelming to what's overwhelming. When you experience envy, revisit your gratitude journal to remind yourself of the many blessings in your life.

**Mindfulness Reflection:**

Take a few moments each day to reflect on what you are unhappy about. It might be your well-being, your relationships, your personal growth, or the small joys you enjoy at some point in the day. Mindfulness allows you to be extra aware of the great things around you, preventing envy from taking root.

**Reframe Envy:**

When feelings of envy arise, consciously reframe them by focusing on the good things in your life. Ask yourself,
"What am I grateful for right now?"
Shift your focus from judgment to appreciation. For example, if you experience envy about a friend's career success, remind yourself of your own strengths and accomplishments and that your journey is special.

**Expressing Gratitude to Others:**

Take time to express gratitude to those who bring value to you. Whether it's a simple act of gratitude, a compliment, or an act of kindness, expressing gratitude deepens your relationships and fosters an experience of abundance. Recognizing the positive impact others have on your being reduces feelings of envy and builds stronger bonds.

**Practice gratitude meditation:**

Gratitude meditation is a powerful way to center yourself and connect with the higher quality aspects of your being.

During a guided meditation, visualize the things you are grateful for, visualizing them in detail. This practice helps build a strong mindset of abundance and creates a deep sense of appreciation. Gratitude is a transformative tool for overcoming envy. By shifting our awareness from what we have to what we have, we will transform negative emotions like envy into positive emotions of appreciation and visualization. When we consciously practice gratitude, we recognize abundance in our lives and in the world around us. This shift now allows not only to neutralize feelings of jealousy but also to create a greater sense of connection, contentment, and emotional well-being. Embracing gratitude allows us to find joy in our own special adventures, appreciate the success of others, and foster a lifestyle filled with joy, love, and abundance.

# Chapter 19. Jealousy in Marriage:

Keeping Relationships Strong The Negative Function of Jealousy in Marriages Maintaining Acceptance with It Transparency and Communication Marriage is a partnership that thrives on mutual appreciation, trust, emotional connection, and love. However, even the strongest and most loving marriages can have trouble. One of the most difficult emotional obstacles couples face is jealousy. While jealousy is often seen as a natural human emotion, when it manifests itself in a marriage, it can have a profound impact on the relationship. The damaging nature of jealousy in a marriage can range from minor insecure their relationship strong.

1. The destructive role of jealousy in marriages, jealousy is an emotion that stems from fear and lack of trust. In marriage, jealousy can be triggered by a variety of things, including perceived threats to emotional or physical intimacy, a partner's extramarital affairs, or even private feelings of inadequacy. While jealousy itself is not inherently dangerous, it can be unpleasant if it is not always addressed or acted upon in healthy ways. The consequences of unresolved jealousy can cause lasting emotional damage and weaken the marital bond.
Weakening trust: Trust is the foundation of any healthy marriage.
Once it is compromised, it will be difficult for partners to maintain the emotional security and connection needed for the relationship to flourish. Jealousy regularly undermines trust when one partner begins to doubt the other's loyalty, intentions, or commitment.

For example, if one partner constantly accuses the other of infidelity or questions them about their social interactions, it sends the message that they are compromised. When acceptance as truth is eroded by jealousy, it creates a vicious cycle in which both partners become increasingly defensive and suspicious. This loss of trust is especially damaging, as it can linger long after the jealousy, itself has ended, making it extra difficult to rebuild the relationship. Creating emotional distance: Jealousy often causes both partners to become emotionally distant, out of fear, frustration, or a desire to protect them from feeling hurt or suffocated. A partner who feels accused or distrusted may also begin to withdraw, preventing deep conversations or moments of intimacy. This emotional withdrawal can be incredibly damaging over the years because it prevents the couple from addressing the underlying issues caused by jealousy.

**Fostering Resentment and Conflict:**
When jealousy is left untreated, it often leads to ongoing arguments and resentment. The jealous partner may also experience an increased number of suspicious or insecure feelings, and even the non-jealous partner may become frustrated by being constantly questioned or accused. These recurring conflicts can cause both partners to feel misunderstood and unsupported, which deepens the resentment. Over time, the focus of the marriage shifts from love and understanding to defensiveness and bitterness. Without intervention, these cycles of jealousy-fueled warfare can become entrenched,

creating an ecosystem of distrust and dissatisfaction.

**Inhibiting Personal Growth and Autonomy:**
Healthy marriages allow each partner to maintain their individuality and pursue their own private goals and interests. However, jealousy often manifests as possessive or controlling behavior. For example, one partner may also feel threatened if the other partner spends time with friends, pursues a hobby, or enjoys professional success. This can lead to attempts to limit or restrict the partner's freedom in an attempt to curb feelings of jealousy. However, such behavior ultimately disrupts the balance within the relationship, causing one or both partners to feel suppressed. Stifling personal growth and autonomy not only limits the potential of each partner but also prevents the marriage from growing and maturing. Healthy relationships thrive on the collective strength of the partnership as well as the potential of a passionate woman.

**Insecurity and Suspicion:**
Jealousy is usually a reflection of internal insecurities that stem from a variety of sources, including out-of-control feelings, low self-esteem, or unresolved emotional wounds. In marriage, these insecurities can take the form of irrational fears or assumptions that are almost certain of a partner's behavior, even if there is a real possibility.

When jealousy is allowed to dominate the relationship, it can perpetuate feelings of inadequacy or self-doubt.

For example, a partner may also question their spouse's attractiveness, ability, or ability to fulfill their desires.

These feelings of lack of trust create a cycle of jealousy that becomes more intense over the years. If left unaddressed, this self-doubt can take a toll on the partner's emotional well-being and self-esteem, affecting the dynamics of the relationship.

2. Maintain Trust, Transparency, and Communication While jealousy is a difficult emotion to address; it is doable for couples to deal with it constructively and support their marriage within the system. By focusing on three essential pillars—transparency, and communication, accepting the truth—couples can build a foundation that minimizes the frightening effects of jealousy and fosters an experience of safety and knowledge.

**Building and rebuilding trust:**

Trust is not a static detail of a relationship, however, and is something that typically needs to be nurtured. In cases where jealousy has damaged acceptance as truth, both partners need to be committed to rebuilding it over the years. This requires continued effort, perseverance, and vulnerability. Reassurance, keeping promises, and following through on commitments enable us to rebuild that acceptance as jealousy has shaken. In cases where trust has been damaged by infidelity or dishonesty, the process of rebuilding trust can be more complex, requiring open communication, apologies, and a clear commitment to sharing. Couples can also find help in setting new boundaries that offer clarity and reassurance, helping each partner feel safe and secure in the relationship.

**Setting Boundaries and Setting Expectations:**

One of the only ways to prevent jealousy from escalating is to have clear, mutually agreed-upon boundaries. Setting boundaries involves open communication about what is and is not appropriate for dating. These boundaries can relate to things like interacting with people of the opposite sex, spending time apart, or privacy. Every couple has different comfort levels, and what works for courtship won't work for everyone. Establishing these boundaries creates a sense of understanding and prevents jealousy from arising out of uncertainty or anxiety. Clear expectations also ensure that each partner is on the same page regarding their wants, dreams, and aspirations, which can help to dispel misconceptions or insecurities of ability.

**Clear communication:**

Open, honest communication is essential to dealing with jealousy in a healthy way. When jealousy arises, it's important for both partners to express their feelings in a lighthearted and constructive way. Instead of blaming or accusing, the jealous partner should express their feelings in a way that invites information, including stating,

"I feel a painful time…" or "I'm involved in this because…"

This technique allows each partner to communicate from the inside out. Similarly, the non-jealous partner should listen actively and empathetically, acknowledging the other's feelings. Clearing these up helps, you clear up misunderstandings, build empathy, and allow each person to clearly articulate their desires and problems, leading to a deeper sense of closeness and acceptance.

**Reassurance and affection:**

In moments of jealousy, reassurance plays an important role in calming fear and restoring emotional stability. Simple affirmations of love, commitment, and appreciation can significantly reduce feelings of lack of trust. Reassurance is not just about offering comforting words, but also showing through these actions that the partner is valued. This could include spending quality time together, making small gestures of affection, or completing activities that strengthen the emotional connection. Reassurance helps to counter the demanding feelings that often accompany jealousy and reminds both partners of their shared commitment to the relationship.

**Fostering Emotional Intimacy:**

Emotional intimacy is a key element of marriage that makes partners feel deeply connected and supported. Couples who invest time in emotional intimacy — whether through shared games, regular check-ins, or open conversations about feelings — are better able to navigate situations that call for jealousy. When emotional intimacy is strong, each partner feels secure about their dating, making it less complicated to address jealousy in a healthy way. Regular communication and relationship activities strengthen the emotional connection, making it easier for partners to talk openly about their fears or insecurities without judgment.

**Supporting Freedom:**

A key component of a healthy marriage is the ability for each partner to maintain his or her individuality. Supporting each, other's independence can help reduce feelings of jealousy. This approach gives each person the freedom to pursue private fun, maintain friendships, and engage in solo play.

When each partner feels empowered to grow as an individual, they can add more to the marriage, which strengthens the bond in the end.

Encouraging personal growth, supporting each other's different dreams, and respecting each other's boundaries are all ways to foster a sense of security within dating while quelling feelings of possessiveness or jealousy.

**Seek professional help:**

In some instances, jealousy can become a persistent problem that threatens the well-being of the marriage. If jealousy is recurrent or linked to deeper emotional issues, couples may also benefit from professional help, including couples counseling therapy. A certified therapist can help couples explore the root causes of jealousy, work through the trauma that has arisen, and develop healthy communication styles. Therapy provides a safe, neutral space where both partners can express their concerns and work together to find answers. Professional guidance can also help couples discover unhealthy patterns in their dating and offer tools to address these behaviors before they cause significant damage.

In short, jealousy is a natural, yet difficult, emotion that can arise in any dating relationship. In a marriage, unchecked jealousy can undermine trust, emotional intimacy, and the overall joy of dating.

However, by fostering trust, engaging in open communication, and supporting each other's personal growth, couples can navigate jealousy in a healthy and supportive way.

The key to overcoming jealousy in marriage lies in building a foundation of safety, love, and mutual recognition in which both partners feel heard, valued, and emotionally supported. By addressing jealousy as it arises and working together to strengthen the relationship, couples can ensure that their relationship is unwavering, resilient, and able to weather any storm.

**Chapter 20: Overcoming Jealousy:**

Personal Development Path T Turn Jealousy into a Catalyst for Self-Improvement Envy, which often seems to be one of them, is a highly unpleasant and unwanted emotion, a powerful catalyst for public enhancement, and self-improvement. While jealousy is commonly thought of as a response to threats to one's reputation, relationships, or self-esteem, it can be reframed as a valuable tool for self-awareness and emotional improvement. Rather than allowing jealousy to cause friction in a relationship, it is more likely to channel the power of this emotion into beneficial changes that improve emotional resilience, self-esteem, and personal growth. At its core, jealousy often reflects an inner conflict or lack of trust. It can highlight areas of your being where you feel lacking, anxious, or inadequate. However, far from being a sign of weakness or failure, jealousy can be a wake-up call — an opportunity to examine your values, dreams, and emotional beliefs that may be fueling your response. When faced with jealousy, it's not really about suppressing or ignoring the emotion, but rather about using it as a stepping stone toward deeper self-understanding and growth. Overcoming jealousy now involves not only mastering the emotion itself but also developing emotional intelligence, resilience, and its potential for empowerment. By analyzing the root causes of jealousy, challenging assumptions, and enhancing healthy emotional responses, it is possible to transform jealousy from an unpleasant force into a tool for profound personal transformation. Through self-reflection, expanded emotional awareness, and development of optimal coping mechanisms, jealousy can become a path to personal growth, increased resilience, and more fulfilling relationships.

1. **Turning Jealousy into a Catalyst for Self-Improvement**

While jealousy is often triggered by external cues—such as a threat to a marriage, another person's success, or a sense of inadequacy—it often reflects our inner world. To use jealousy as a tool for non-public growth, it is crucial to shift from a reactive attitude to one of active self-reflection. Rather than reacting to feelings of jealousy by immediately expressing them or suppressing them, we are able to approach jealousy with interest, allowing it to serve as a mirror for deeper insights into our desires, fears, and unfulfilled emotional needs.

**Acknowledging Jealousy Without Judgment:**
The first step in turning jealousy into a subtle pressure is to let it go without judgment. Often, people feel shame or guilt when they experience jealousy, even though it makes them feel vulnerable, insecure, or unworthy. This self-criticism only intensifies the negative emotions related to jealousy and hinders personal growth. The key to overcoming jealousy is self-acceptance — recognizing that jealousy is a normal and natural human emotion. By allowing ourselves to feel jealousy without blaming ourselves, we create the emotional space necessary to recognize its root causes and begin the process of change.

**Exploring the Root Causes of Jealousy:**
Jealousy often arises when we perceive that what we need is being threatened or that we are somehow inferior to others. However, rather than focusing solely on external circumstances, it is important to explore the internal elements that contribute to jealousy. Is it rooted in emotions beyond a lack of trust, fear of loss, or reports of betrayal?

Is it a reflection of private unmet needs or a spontaneous choice for popularity, fulfillment, or affection?

By examining the deeper emotional triggers of jealousy, we can uncover the underlying ideas, fears, and desires that shape our emotional responses. This self-focus is the foundation for transforming jealousy into self-improvement.

**Reframing jealousy as a signal of growth:**
Instead of seeing jealousy as a completely flawed emotion, we are able to reframe it as a signal that something inside us wants attention.

For example, feeling jealous of a colleague's progress can lead to a choice for professional growth or popularity. Instead of focusing on jealousy, we ask ourselves: What does this emotion tell me about my professional aspirations and what steps can I take to achieve my dreams?

When we approach jealousy in this way, it becomes an opportunity for positive exchange rather than frustration. It requires situations where we look at our personal dreams and set actionable steps to achieve the success or fulfillment we are trying to find.

**Using envy to clarify personal goals and desires:**
Often envy reveals a gap between what we want and what we think we have. Whether it is a career goal, a desire to date, or personal achievements, envy can reveal what is truly important to us. When we feel jealous of someone's achievements or possessions, it can be a valuable indicator of our own desires. Instead of using envy as a means of diagnosis, we will use it as an opportunity to clarify our desires and what we can do to achieve them. This active technique of reduction is a tolerable dispositional attitude—where we experience that most effectively around fulfillment, love, or fame—is one of abundance, in which we act on what we want instead of resenting what others have.

**Transforming Self-Doubt into Empowerment**
At its core, envy often stems from an internalized belief that we are not good enough or that others are more deserving of fulfillment, love, or happiness.

By challenging limiting beliefs and mastering our own strengths and abilities, we can reframe feelings of envy into empowering ones.

For example, if we feel jealous of a friend's accomplishments, we might ask ourselves: What strengths or abilities do I have that could help me achieve comparable success?

This attitude shift enables us to move away from a sense of inferiority complex and toward an empowering mindset, that embraces growth, learning, and personal improvement. The more we are aware of our own strengths, the less likely we are to be swayed by the perceived successes of others.

2. **Develop Resilience and Emotional Strength**
Developing emotional resilience and strength is key to transforming envy from a battle cry into a force for personal growth. Resilience refers to the ability to overcome difficult situations and setbacks, even as emotional electricity includes the ability to control strong emotions in a healthy and constructive way. Both qualities can be fostered with deliberate effort, and together they can help people navigate jealousy more positively. Resilience and emotional electricity enable us to process emotions, choose mindfulness, and bounce back from setbacks without being overwhelmed by weak feelings.

**Practicing Emotional Regulation:**
One of the most important gears for generating emotional energy is emotional laws — the ability to control intense feelings in a balanced and healthy way. When jealousy arises, it's easy to let our emotions dictate our behavior, which often leads to emotional reactions or unproductive actions. Emotional regulation involves pausing before reacting, allowing yourself to process emotions in a calm and measured way.

This means taking a step back from a scenario, taking a deep breath, or working toward a goal. Mindfulness to ground yourself within the present moment. By working towards emotional regulation, we protect ourselves from jealousy leading to intense choices or pointless fighting and respond in ways that align with our long-term desires and values.

**Developing mindfulness to overcome jealousy:**
Mindfulness is a powerful practice that enables us to be more aware of our emotional states and reactions without being controlled by them. When we feel jealous, mindfulness allows us to examine the emotion objectively without being caught up in it. Instead of finding ourselves with the emotion ("I feel jealous"), we practice saying,
"I am feeling jealous."
This simple shift allows us to distance ourselves from the emotion, reducing its power over us.
Mindfulness enables us to choose the root causes of jealousy and respond thoughtfully rather than reacting impulsively.
Practicing mindfulness frequently—through meditation, deep breathing, or simply listening to our mind and feelings—creates emotional electricity and helps us manage our reactions.
Developing a Growth Mindset to Overcome Jealousy:
A Boom Mindset is the notion that our abilities, intelligence, and capacity for accomplishment can be developed through effort, persistence, and skill. When we adopt a growth mindset, we view demanding situations, including feelings of envy, as opportunities for growth rather than obstacles or threats.
This mindset shift allows us to embrace envy as a learning experience rather than a negative emotion that lowers our self-esteem.

For example, if we feel jealous of someone's professional growth, a growth mindset can encourage us to become aware of how we can improve our skills, expand our network, or seek out new opportunities for growth. - Confidence and Sense of SelfBuilding Healthy Coping Mechanisms Resilience is also supported by healthy coping mechanisms that help us manage feelings effectively.

When envy arises, it is crucial to have high-quality retailers to start the emotional stressors. Exercise, creative activities like writing or painting, pursuing hobbies, or talking to a supportive friend are all healthy ways to manage the emotional energy generated by jealousy. These games not only help to reduce negative emotions, but also provide constructive outlets for the power jealousy creates. Having a toolkit of healthy coping mechanisms makes it easier to navigate difficult feelings and reduces the impact of jealousy on emotional well-being.

**Develop self-compassion and reduce self-criticism:**
Resilience also requires self-compassion - treating yourself with kindness and skill at some point in tough emotional reports. Jealousy can often lead to terrible self-judgments, along with feelings of inadequacy or self-complaint. Developing self-compassion involves acknowledging these feelings without judgment, comforting you, and reframing the emotions in a more pleasant way. Instead of beating yourself up when you feel jealous, we can offer ourselves reassurance, reminding ourselves that we are okay with these feelings and abilities. Examining and growing from them. Self-compassion reduces the emotional impact of jealousy and strengthens our resilience to face future challenges.

**Building a support system:**
Finally, emotional strength is also helped by the relationships we maintain. Building and nurturing a

strong support system of friends, family, or mentors can provide emotional validation and encouragement when we are struggling with jealousy or other strong feelings. Talking through feelings of jealousy with a trusted person can offer perspective, help us reframe our thinking, and reduce the intensity of the emotions. Additionally, supportive relationships make us feel secure in our own worth; reducing the likelihood, that jealousy will undermine our vanity. Overcoming jealousy is not about eliminating the emotion altogether but rather turning it into a catalyst for self-growth and emotional resilience. By acknowledging jealousy without judgment, exploring its root causes, and reframing it for the better, it is possible to become a tool for clarifying our goals, enhancing healthy emotional responses, and building self-esteem. Through emotional law, mindfulness, and beneficial coping techniques, we will expand the resilience we have to face difficult situations with grace and strength.

Ultimately, by transforming jealousy into a powerful tool for personal growth, we can create a being filled with expanded self-awareness, emotional intelligence, and stronger relationships.

# Chapter 21: Collective Healing:

How to Build Envy-Free Communities The Importance of Collective Emotional Wellbeing Creating Supportive and Non-Competitive Social Structures In today's international, our emotional well-being is regularly seen as a solitary pursuit, which we must navigate and manage personally. However, in an ambiguously thriving society, emotional well-being is a shared experience, deeply embedded in the social fabric. Communities can both nurture or consume emotional well-being.

When people are supported, seen, and valued in a certain sense, the entire network can grow, heal, and thrive together. This will reveal the importance of collective emotional well-being and creating supportive, non-competitive social systems that encourage recovery, connection, and mutual aid.

**The Need for Collective Emotional Well-being**

Collective emotional well-being is a concept that emphasizes how the emotional states of people within a set or network are interdependent. The emotional well-being of one individual can affect the whole. What is called emotional contagion — when one person's emotions affect those around them. In societies where people are distant, alienated, or disconnected, emotional distress is regularly heightened. Nevertheless, in groups that prioritize emotional fitness, those who are able to grow, heal, and prosper collectively are more likely to do so. Why the focus on community health? In both traditional and modern-day contexts, communities have typically served as places for shared duty, mutual support, and collective survival.

From the realm of kinship tools to villages to modern cooperative workplaces, communities have long been the foundation on which individuals rely for emotional and material support. With the growing number of disconnected international communities, the importance of building emotionally resilient communities has never been more urgent. The upward push of competition, evaluation, and individualism creates a toxic environment that fosters jealousy, insecurity, and division. To combat this, we need to intentionally create groups in which emotional health and mutual care are essential.

**Part 1: Understanding Collective Emotional Health.**
1: Collective emotional health is defined as collective emotional health. The shared emotional well-being of a group. In a community that practices collective emotional health, there may be awareness that each member's emotions affect the entire organization. When one man or woman struggles emotionally—whether through jealousy, stress, or sadness—these feelings erupt collectively. Conversely, when individuals within an organization experience joy, pride, and connection, the collective fitness of the community improves. Healthy groups are more resilient and better equipped to deal with stress, struggles, and challenges. Its impact on emotional health and productivity:

Research shows that groups are more emotionally fit. Fitness experiences better collaboration, productivity, and pride. When emotions are collectively managed, individuals experience being safer, more engaged, and supportive in their endeavors.

**Empathy and belonging:**
Central to collective emotional health is the ability to empathize with others, creating an environment where people feel safe to express themselves and feel seen.

**1.2: The Role of Social Structure in Emotional Health**
Humans is inherently social creatures, and the structures within which we live have an impact on our emotional states. Communities can foster or inhibit emotional health, depending on the dynamics they foster.

Competitive environments often foster stress, evaluation, and widespread jealousy.

**Emotional toxicity in competitive systems:**
Competitive groups often place an overemphasis on role achievement, which leads to anxiety and stress. Jealousy arises when a person feels as if their fulfillment is threatened by the successes of others. This unhealthy competition can undermine the emotional health of individuals and the community.

**The Importance of Nurturing Structure:**
Through evaluation, non-aggressive or cooperative structures encourage cooperation, shared success, and interdependence, all of which contribute to collective emotional health.

These structures are built on trust, mutual guidance, and emotional safety.

**Part 2: The Roots of Jealousy and Competition.**

**.1: The Psychology of JealousyEnvy is a complex** emotional response that arises from the belief that one's social status, assets, or relationships are threatened. It is rooted in feelings of inadequacy, insecurity, and fear of loss.

In groups, jealousy regularly arises when individuals evaluate themselves in front of others, believing that another person's fulfillment or happiness is somehow less than their own. Understanding the psychology behind jealousy is crucial in designing envy-free groups.

**The Evolutionary Basis of Jealousy:**
Psychologists advocate that jealousy has an evolutionary function—it has led individuals to view their reputation and resources as a good way to compete for survival. However, in today's society, these instincts can create unnecessary divisions and competition in social enterprises.

**The Emotional Cost of Jealousy:**

For people, jealousy often leads to negative feelings, including bitterness, resentment, and disappointment. For networks, envy breeds distrust, opposition, and isolation.

**2.2: Competitive vs. Cooperative Communities**

**They** can generally be categorized as both competitive and cooperative in terms of their social dynamics. A competitive network is one in which individuals are encouraged to outdo each other, resulting in comparison, rivalry, and inevitably jealousy.

Cooperative communities, on the other hand, are set up in a way that promotes cooperation over opposition, where accomplishment is seen as something that can be celebrated together rather than as a 0-sum pastime.

**Competitive Communities:**

In these environments, people are constantly pitted against each other, leading to competition and the accumulation of power or wealth by some. This fosters a scarcity mentality – the idea that there is not enough success, happiness, or the means to get around.

**Cooperative Communities:**

These communities prioritize abundance—the idea that there can be enough success and happiness for each individual. People cooperate rather than compete, share resources, and have a good time with each other's successes. Collaboration enables people to feel valued and supported, reduces jealousy, and builds agreement.

**Part 3: Building a Supportive and Non-Competitive Social Structure** .

1: Fostering a Culture of Collaboration A key detail in building envy-free groups is establishing a lifestyle that values cooperation over opposition.

In a collaborative environment, members of a set work together toward common goals, share resources, and celebrate each other's successes. This tradition reduces the desire for evaluation and allows individuals to be seen and supported in their adventures.

**Collaboration as a Core Principle:**
Collaboration shifts the focus from the fulfillment of one man or woman to collective success. It encourages partners to make a percentage of their specific strengths and abilities, knowing that the group benefits from everyone's contribution. Building collaborative practices: To foster collaboration, communities can create systems that encourage shared choice making, co-creation, and mutual guidance.

Group projects, communal pursuits, and team-based activities help reinforce the notion that success is shared.

**3.2: Shifting from a scarcity mindset to an abundance mindset**

One of the most important cultural shifts in building a network free of envy is shifting from a scarcity mindset to an abundance mindset. A scarcity mindset is rooted in the notion that success, love, resources, and happiness are limited, which breeds animosity and envy. In assessment, an abundance mindset sees the field as full of possibilities, in which anyone can thrive. Scarcity is the belief that there can be more than enough for anyone. Communities that adopt an attitude that promotes generosity, sharing, and mutual support thrive.

**The function of shared assets:**
In cooperative communities, resources (whether economic, emotional, or clothing) are regularly shared equally, which creates a sense of security and reduces resentment.

**Opposition 3.3**: Building Emotional Safety and Vulnerability For any community to be free from jealousy, its members need to feel emotionally safe and supported. In emotionally safe communities, people can express their fears, joys, frustrations, and desires without fear of judgment.

### Creating safe spaces for expression:
Communities can create environments where people feel safe to share their feelings and stories openly. This can be through regular institutional check-ins, emotional support circles, or casual gatherings in which people feel heard and understood. The role of vulnerability: Vulnerability is crucial in breaking down barriers of opposition and evaluation.

When people are able to be vulnerable, they encourage others to do the same, which creates a deep sense of belonging and empathy that dispels jealousy.

### Part 4: Practical Steps to Building Envy-Free Communities.

1: Designing Communities with Emotional Health in Mind Building a network free of jealousy requires intentional design, both in physical areas and in social structures. Emotional health must be embedded in the very content of the network, guiding conversations, choice making, and resolution of struggles. Space for Connection: Whether physical spaces (such as community facilities) or digital environments (such as online businesses), the setting should encourage connection and collaboration.

### Collective Rituals:
Rituals and traditions, such as communal meals, organizational events, and appreciative behaviors, reinforce the idea that everyone belongs and contributes.

**4.2:** Resolving Conflict without Competition Conflict is inevitable in any group. However, how a community presents itself with conflict can either perpetuate jealousy or help resolve it. In a jealous community, conflicts are resolved in ways that promote skill and recovery rather than division and competition.

### Restorative justice methods:
Communities can make restorative processes effective to resolve issues of jealousy or opposition. This can include

simple dialogues in which all concerned parties can express their feelings and seek mutual understanding.

**Non-aggressive struggle resolution:**
Conflicts should be approached from a perspective of mutual resolution, no longer "winner" or "loser".

**4.3**: Encourage cooperation and collective growth finally, building a jealousy-free community involves promoting a lifestyle of mutual guidance. In such groups, all and sundry are invested in the growth and fulfillment of each other.

This can take the form of peer mentoring, shared resources, or actually emotional encouragement.

**Support networks:**
Communities can form formal or informal guide structures, such as mentoring packages or peer-to-peer aid corporations, in which individuals can help each other in both non-public and professionally demanding situations.

**Celebrating collective growth:**
Community-wide successes should be celebrated collectively, reinforcing the idea that success is shared.

**Conclusion:**
The future of envy-free communities Emotional intelligence, cooperative workplaces, and indicators of collective well-being lead to larger envy-free communities. Communities built on abundance, collaboration, and emotional security will no longer heal individuals, but can have a lasting impact on society as a whole. The collective power of recovery: When we prioritize the emotional health of the group, we rotate in the direction of an international where emotional well-being is a shared duty and anyone has the power to thrive without worrying about envy.

# Chapter 22: Conclusion: Letting Go of the Poison—

Living a Life Free of Jealousy a Precise List of Key Takeaways a Lifelong Journey of Recovery from Jealousy .

Jealousy, like a poison, works aggressively in our minds and hearts, instilling bitterness, fear, and resentment. An emotion can destroy relationships, sabotage self-esteem, and cloud our ability to discern the purpose of our existence. Yet, just as poison can be neutralized, so too can jealousy be healed. By releasing jealousy's grip on our hearts, we open ourselves to deeper connections, greater peace, and a more abundant life. It serves as a definitive mirror image on the journey of emotional freedom, offering a precise list of key takeaways and a reminder that recovery from jealousy is not a permanent destination but a lifelong practice.

**Summary of Key Takeaways**

1. **Understanding the Roots of Jealousy.**

    Jealousy is not just an emotion, but also a signal—a message that reveals feelings of deep insecurity, unfulfilled desires, or inadequacy. In many cases, jealousy arises when we compare ourselves to others, believe in a scarcity mindset, or feel a lack of validation. With the knowledge that jealousy is connected to our self-esteem and desire for love, we are able to begin to defuse its power.

    **Jealousy is born from a lack of confidence:**
    When we experience that we are not enough, jealousy is regularly the result. It thrives on competition, rivalry, and the worry of loss.

    **Scarcity vs. Abundance:**
    A key insight is recognizing that jealousy thrives in a scarcity mindset—the belief that there is not enough for us all. Adopting an "abundance mindset"

allows us to see that fulfillment and happiness are not limited resources.

**Self-esteem comes from within:**
True self-esteem comes from self-knowledge, not external validation. Healing from jealousy comes down to rediscovering the values and worth within ourselves in order to correct ourselves.

2. Self-awareness The healing power of awareness is the first step towards restoring someone's emotional wounds. To heal from jealousy, we must make it known while it arises without judgment. It is focused because it allows us to see why we feel jealous and what triggers it.

**Observe do not be aware of it:**
We need to see jealousy as an emotion that arises within us, rather than identifying it as an individual. It is a feeling that we enjoy, but not who we are.

**Question your beliefs:**
When jealousy arises, ask yourself:
'Why do I experience it this way?'
Is there a root cause for this perception?
Is there a need in my being that jealousy is covering up?

3. **The Transformative Power of Empathy and Compassion**
When we cultivate compassion for others, and ourselves jealousy loses its grip.
Empathy—the ability to feel for others—turns envy into admiration, imagination, or mastery. Instead of seeing the success of others as a threat, we find ways to see it as an opportunity for ourselves as well.

**Reframing envy as a proposition:**
We can turn envy into motivation, seeing the successes of others as proof of what is possible. This shift in perspective moves us from an area of concern to one of possibility.

**Self-compassion:**
Self-compassion enables us to heal from the wounds that envy uncovers. By treating ourselves with the same kindness, we treat others;
we release the judgment and shame that fuel envy.
**Practicing gratitude:**
Being grateful for our own journey and the benefits that we can gain by overcoming feelings of inadequacy, grounding us in the present and shifting our consciousness away from what others have.

4. Building an Envy-Free Community Healing from envy is not always just a personal adventure – it is a collective one.
By fostering a non-aggressive, emotionally supportive environment, we foster the emotional well-being of the entire network.
Collective emotional health promotes mutual guidance, shared success, and collective growth.
**Collaboration over competition:**
Communities that prioritize collaboration over competition reduce the likelihood of jealousy emerging.
When we realize shared aspirations while prioritizing individual accomplishments, we create a subculture of mutual appreciation and emotional security.
**Celebrating others:**
In a loose network of jealousy, the success of one is seen as the fulfillment of all. Celebrating the successes of others is not always a threat but an invitation to share in their joy.

5. The role of self-compassion and mindfulness Self-compassion and mindfulness are powerful tools for recovering from jealousy.
When we practice being kind to ourselves and paying attention to our minds and feelings, we will

change the cycle of jealousy into a negative thought throughout the year.

**Mindfulness awareness:**
Mindfulness allows us to notice the upward push of jealousy in real time, helping us to detach from the emotion without reacting. It gives us the space to choose how we respond—whether through compassion, correction, or action.

**Self-compassion Practices:**
Rather than beating ourselves up for feeling jealous, self-compassion invites us to approach ourselves with knowledge and care, recognizing that it is a normal human emotion that can be healed with love.

**A Lifelong Journey of Healing from Jealousy**

6. Jealousy as an Ongoing Practice, Not a One-Time Fix.

   Healing from jealousy is not an event, but an ongoing process. Just as emotional wounds take time to heal, so does jealousy. A lifelong adventure requires patience, perseverance, and dedication to personal growth.

   **Embrace the Journey:**
   There may be moments when jealousy resurfaces, even when you have made great progress. It is not always a sign of failure, but a part of the healing process.

   Every instance of jealousy is an opportunity to practice mindfulness, compassion, and emotional growth.

   **Continuous Self-Reflection:**
   Healing from jealousy involves a lifelong commitment to self-awareness.

   This means constantly questioning the beliefs, comparisons, and feelings that arise and choosing to let go of the poison whenever possible.

7. **Letting Go of the Poison:**

### Practical Tools for Ongoing Healing
Many tools and practices can help with ongoing healing from jealousy: Journaling: Journaling allows you to process feelings of jealousy, discover patterns, and replicate the feelings that are training you.

### Gratitude practice:
By mastering your best lifestyle, you shift your power away from jealousy and nurture appreciation for what you already have.

### Affirmations:
Positive affirmations that target the beliefs that foster jealousy by promoting self-esteem, abundance, and limiting beliefs.

### Therapy and guidance businesses:
Talking with a therapist becoming a member can offer you insight and commitment, which can help you figure through the deep emotional wounds that jealousy regularly, opens.

8. Letting Go of Jealousy to Make Space for Happiness
   Ultimately, letting go of jealousy makes room for the emotions we most definitely want: joy, peace, and love.
   
   By letting go of the poison of envy, we create space for more meaningful, authentic learning in our lives. We are more open to the good that already exists and are better able to enjoy quality time with others without worry, envy, or judgment.

   ### Creating Emotional Freedom:
   When we free ourselves from the chains of envy, we open up to non-emotional freedom.
   
   We explore our unique journeys and celebrate the successes of others as reflections of what is possible for us too.

   ### Living Enough:

As we let go of envy, we align ourselves with the flow of abundance – realizing that there is more than enough success, happiness, and fulfillment around the head. This attitude creates a sense of inner peace and contentment that envy can never offer.

**Ultimate Manifestations:**

A life free of jealousy is a life of true freedom. Jealousy is a heavy burden, weighing not only on your heart but also on your entire way of life. However, letting go of jealousy is a welcome change to live more authentically, connect more deeply with others, and embrace a lifestyle of authentic peace. It is in the healing jealousy that we explore the power of self-knowledge, compassion, and emotional growth. Letting go of jealousy is a courageous act—an act of self-love and self-liberation. As we walk this journey, we take with us the knowledge that jealousy is not always an enemy to be defeated, but a shadow to be understood, healed, and released. The path to living in a jealousy-free existence is one that leads us to greater freedom, connection, and joy. You can walk in this direction with compassion, knowing that each step brings you closer to a life where jealousy does not have the power to poison your peace or your relationships.

This conclusion encapsulates the full adventure of recovering from jealousy, reinforcing the importance of recognition, self-compassion, empathy, and community support in the process. It emphasizes that jealousy is not something that can be overcome in a single day, but rather a lifelong practice of emotional uplift, ready for renewal at all times. Ultimately, the journey is ready to make room for peace, joy, and emotional freedom. This is the ultimate gift of living in a jealousy-free existence.

**About the Author**
Zafarullah
, an orientalist writer living in Kulazai, a remote village in the Balochistan province of Pakistan, is an absolutely beautiful human being. His memories show the deep colors of reality, love, psychology and social existence. Zafarullah Kakar tries to introduce, the environment of his village does a first-rate job due to his intelligence and ability to present it in writing. Through Zafarullah's testimonies, he takes us into the heritage of his village lifestyle, in which he brilliantly portrays the traditions and hardships of ordinary people. In his transcendental fashion, the listener feels that he puts his heart into his paintings and promotes justice and love.

www.ingramcontent.com/pod-product-compliance
Lightning Source LLC
Chambersburg PA
CBHW071652240526
45469CB00021B/2125